PACKED WITH BEST HOLIS
NUTRITIONAL EATING & COO

So *soul* EASY VEGAN RECIPES

OVER 100 QUICK RECIPES TO HEAL & NOURISH YOUR BODY, MIND & *Soul*

JAYANTHI BOMMANA

CERTIFIED YOGA INSTRUCTOR, PLANT-BASED NUTRITION & HOLISTIC LIFESTYLE MENTOR

First Printing, 2024
ISBN - 978-1-915857-04-0 (Paperback)
ISBN - 978-1-915857-05-7 (eBook)
ISBN - 978-1-915857-06-4 (Hardback)

in association with

in aid of

10% of the profit from this book is donated to the Holistic Health Movement.

In Gratitude

I am eternally grateful...

To my mother and father for instilling the foundation of balanced nourishment.

To my sister for her joyful companionship along with constant motivation.

To my husband and children for their unwavering support to walk my unique path.

To my mentors Shri Srinivasa Chowdary Alluri, Grandmaster Prabodh Achyutha Musipatla, Mr Sharad Kumar Patil for igniting inner wisdom on holistic wellbeing.

To my book mentor & publisher Ritesh S Nigam for giving life to the simple recipes with his thoughtful ideas, guidance and support in every step.

And finally, to my community of friends for supporting this humble work with encouragement.

AN AYURVEDIC PROVERB

When our diet is wrong, medicine is of no use; when diet is correct, medicine is of no need.

Contents
at a Glance

Contents

Introduction

Raw Detox Drinks

Contents

Raw Smoothies

Warm Beverages & Plant-based Milk

Raw Sprouts & Salads

Contents

Contents

Steamed Soups & Veggies

Cooked Whole Grain Meals

Contents

contd.. Cooked Whole Grain Meals

Recovery Remedies

Nutrients Key & Charts

You are what you eat

UPANISHADS & INDIAN VEDAS

Author's Note

A lifetime appreciation for fresh, home-cooked meals laid the foundation for my journey into the world of healthy plant-based cuisine.

I grew up in India, where my mother prepared fresh food daily, carrying homemade dishes in tow to fuel our family, even on long trips.

She was my first influence, my first culinary teacher, who showed eating fresh from the earth is a joy and natural, not a chore.

Years later, as an adult living in UK, balancing family life, motherhood and social life, my diet shifted more towards quick convenience and western lifestyle. Like many, I struggled with post-pregnancy weight gain and the gnawing sense that something wasn't right.

It wasn't until discovering the power of natural wholesome food through a chance community workshop that everything changed.

I was then fortunate to have come into contact with a great humanitarian, Shri Srinivasa Alluri who ignited into me the power of eating wholesome foods along with yoga to understand our body better and treat it like a temple.

Incorporating more vegetables, fruits, legumes and whole grains while adopting a vegetarian and then vegan lifestyle transformed my health in noticeable ways. With abundant energy, effortless weight management, and an overall sense of vitality, I became a true believer in the nutritional & medicinal magic of eating more plants.

Witnessing similar transformations amongst family and friends as I shared this lifestyle, it became clear just how many suffer from preventable illnesses simply due to lack of nutrition awareness.

Equipped with scientific knowledge on the healing properties of plant-based wholefoods, I felt called to help others unlock the transformative power of plant-based holistic eating & cooking.

The result is this collection of recipes focused on flavour and function. I aim to simplify healthy plant-based satvic cooking with Soul Easy Vegan recipes that check every box when it comes to nourishing your Body, Mind & Soul.

With love and joy..

Jayanthi

CERTIFIED YOGA INSTRUCTOR,
PLANT-BASED NUTRITION &
HOLISTIC LIFESTYLE MENTOR

My Holistic View of Food

Is There a Sacred Purpose Behind Every Bite, Lets explore!!

Why Do We Eat?

For years, like many, I saw food merely as fuel, shovelling in meals to pacify hunger between non-stop work and parenting. Stress-eating when anxious and busy. Mindlessly grazed when bored. But my health issues became a wake up call to rethink my relationship with food.

I realised every meal carries a higher purpose - nourishing not just the physical body, but subtle energy channels that animate spirit, creativity, our deepest self. Ancient traditions viewed food as sacred medicine with potency to heal, ground and transform consciousness. Through thoughtful and holistic eating, we can unleash our greatest potential and carve a path to reach our goals.

When Should We Eat?

Rushing between tasks, I'd slam meals down quickly without tuning into genuine hunger or digestion signals. I began checking in more - am I truly ready to receive more fuel or still processing earlier nutrients?

I started spacing meals to allow full assimilation, avoiding overlapping digestion. This honours the body's innate rhythms, governed by forces far wiser than our busyness. Just as moon cycles guide tides, meals synchronised to metabolic signals optimise wellness. Stress hormones dysregulated digestion, so taking time to metabolise each meal benefits every system.

I also integrate one day water-fasting per week - an ancient cleansing tradition that research shows activates beneficial cellular processes like autophagy, digestion resetting and immune regeneration.

"Langanam Parama-Aushadham" - Fasting is a great medicine
A Sanskrit Quote

What Do We Eat?

Of course with such immense power over health comes responsibility in wielding food thoughtfully. My wellness, cognition, and inflammation levels are directly tied to cumulative dietary choices - for better or worse.

I dove into research on the medicinal properties hiding within ordinary plants, stunned by antioxidants, anti-cancer compounds and protective chemicals unmatched by any pharmaceutical. Feed cells a rainbow of fresh, organic produce daily and nutrients will synthesise the miracle medicine we need from within.

How Do We Eat?

Ever finish a meal staring at the screen barely aware of eating? Consuming lunch en route to another task? When we consume food absentminded, the molecular signals activating digestion get disrupted.

I began carving out 20 minutes, sit cross-leg and savour meals slowly, focusing exclusively on each bite. Taking pauses mid-meal once feeling moderately full to let satiation signals arise, preventing overeating. This mindful eating amplified enjoyment and boosted assimilation significantly.

It is important to eat the right food at the right time for efficient digestion. An interval of minimum three to 4 hours between each meal is necessary. It's best to eat only when we feel hungry and drink when thirsty listening to body's cues and stopping to eat when 80% full. Taking a short break after consuming food (before getting back to daily chores) is best for aiding good digestion.

Drinking water immediately before, during and after meals is not advisable as it depletes the digestive fire. Stopping to drink 30 mins before meals, avoiding until 60-90 minutes after food is best for ideal digestion.

The story continues as I share insights on curating a holistic plant-based diet and adopting rituals that infuse deeper meaning into meals. But I hope I've revealed to you, just as was revealed to me - we have an extraordinary opportunity waiting at nearly every table.

The Holistic Principles of Eating

Food is so much more than just fuel. Every bite contains the life force needed to nourish our cells, organs and subtle energies. When we view eating as a sacred act, it transforms our health in profound ways.

The Purpose of Eating

"We are living in abundance, but are we living abundantly?" I find myself asking this as I watch people mindlessly grazing for emotional relief rather than intentional nourishment. Stress eating and overindulgence in empty calories depletes our vitality.

I believe our purpose of eating is to prepare ourselves to reach higher consciousness by consuming high quality nutrients holistically, rather than thoughtlessly filling some void. We must eat to live, not live to eat. This perspective shift is key to harnessing food's incredible power to heal and energise.

Introducing Plant-Based Holistic Eating

A plant-based or Vegan diet based on whole foods resonates most with our bodies' needs and our planet's health. And adopting holistic eating principles amplifies the benefits exponentially.

Holistic eating considers the medicinal properties, elemental qualities, seasonal appropriateness, location grown and ripeness of ingredients. It's a practice rooted in listening inwardly to what your unique constitution requires for balance and contentment in that meal.

The Nutrition and Medicinal Benefits of Plant-Based Foods

Plants offer a complex matrix of antioxidants, anti-inflammatory compounds, detoxifying fibres and protective phytochemicals unmatched in any other foods. Consuming a rainbow of fresh, ripe produce daily is the most direct path towards flooding cells with nourishing compounds that heal and strengthen us from within.

SOUL EASY VEGAN RECIPES

Incorporating all Five Elements for Balance

Plant foods also embody the five elements - earth, water, fire, air and space. Consciously choosing ingredients from each elemental category promotes greater balance and vitality.

Ancient Indian meal system with all the six tastes

Everything we eat has a certain taste and that taste has specific actions on the body and mind when the food comes in contact with our tongue. The six tastes - sweet, sour, salty, pungent, bitter and astringent stimulate a particular bodily organ and it's important to activate all the organs for proper functioning.

When we take in food with all six tastes, food will become our medicine and the body will be very grateful for aiding a healthy digestion. Thus meals present beautifully complex opportunities to holistically realign the five elements within through six tastes! Carefully curating plant palettes lets us orchestrate harmony between our inner and outer worlds like a balanced composition.

A nutritious melody of elements and flavours across meals and seasons keeps organs humming, systems singing! Disease manifests when elements waver out of tune over time through nutritional deficiencies. But eyes, skin and vitality glow radiantly when properly nourished!

Knowing the connection between the five elements, six tastes, higher consciousness with respect to food helps us achieve the highest energy levels to live a long and healthy life.

> *āhāras tv api sarvasya tri-vidho bhavati priyah*
> *yajñas tapas tathā dānaṁ teṣhāṁ bhedam imaṁ śhṛṇu*
>
> **THE FOOD ONE EATS AND HIS PERSONALITY ARE RELATED**
>
> **BHAGAVAD GITA: CHAPTER 17, VERSE 7**

The Holistic Principles of Cooking

Cooking Temperature

Raw Plant-based food has abundant enzymes, nutrients & antioxidants essential for health, but for some recipes cooking is needed and it is recommended to cook approx under 115°F or 45°C.

Downsides of Cooking Above 115°F or 45°C

- Temperatures over 115°Fcor 45°C start to damage enzymes and nutrients
- Food becomes more acidic lacking natural benefits
- Can rob the body's own enzyme reserves during digestion
- Longterm, may contribute to deficient health

Cooking with Suitable Vessel

- Clay: Excellent for heat and nutrient retention but requires more care.
- Cast iron: Second best, good for heat retention and iron absorption, but avoid acidic foods due to potential leaching and bitterness. Minimal maintenance needed.
- Ceramic, ceramic coated cast iron or steel are good options too. Many people prefer heavy bottomed stainless steel for ease of maintenance.

Note: Aluminium and non-stick cookware is best avoided as it build up toxins when food is cooked causing long term health issues.

Storage Vessels

- Earthenware and bell metal: Traditionally considered ideal for storage.
- Glass: Preferred modern option for its inertness and ease of cleaning.

Note: But never store food in plastic containers. Hot food or any stored food added in plastic containers becomes toxic by leakage of chemicals from plastic and is found to cause health problems from reproductive issues to diabetes, obesity etc.

Serving Plates

- Banana leaf: Traditional Indian option believed to to have medicinal properties and antioxidants, enhances flavour and boost digestive health.
- Gold or silver plates: Used historically in India.
- Metal plates: Generally safe, especially compared to plastic. Avoid plastic containers for hot food due to potential leaching of harmful chemicals.

Thoroughly Washing Ingredients

It is important to properly clean all vegetables, fruits, and grains before cooking. If using non-organic produce, aim to soak in a dilute baking soda solution for 10-15 minutes then rinse to remove pesticides residues before prepping dishes. Choosing organic is ideal for avoiding chemical exposures from the start.

Cooking in a Conscious, Positive State

The emotional vibration embedded into dishes while cooking deeply matters. Prepare food while cultivating inner peace through mantras, music or meditative breaths. Studies show one's energetic state interacts at a nutrient level, later influencing the meal's consumers.

Studies validate that our emotional states directly pass into meals, later influencing those who eat. Dishes made with stress breed more distress. Meals prepared in joy awaken more joy. Conscious awareness infuses recipes with flavor that satisfies hearts even more than bellies.

Gently approach your kitchen as a sanctuary brimming with potential for positive manifestation. Allow your core essence and wisdom to flow through your hands into each dish, using cooking as a way to spread good into the world with love behind every movement.

While science and ancient wisdom based holistic plant-based food offers proper nutrition, never overlook the intuitive art of cooking itself as healing transformation.

This is the central idea behind this book - Soul Easy Vegan Recipes.

Decoding Myths about Vegan Lifestyle

Myth: We need meat for sufficient protein
Plants provide easily absorbed protein without overburdening our body's filtration capacity. Adequacy comes from an assortment of beans, lentils, greens and nuts.

Myth: More protein equals greater strength
Excess protein stresses organs and lymphatic system. Moderation with plants provides what we need without unwanted side effects.

Myth: Generous oil makes meals tastier
Our body optimally thrives on the small amounts of beneficial fats naturally occurring in nuts, seeds and avocados when eaten whole. Additional oil is unnecessary and it also removes the original taste of the ingredients.

Myth: Must avoid carboydrates to lose weight
Our cells rely on slow-burning complex carbs from whole grains, legumes and starchy produce for sustained, balanced energy. These nourish in moderation.

Myth: Supplements are vital if eating vegan
A colorful array of whole, fresh, organic plant foods supplies all required vitamins and minerals when skillfully combined and eaten regularly.

Myth: Calorie math ensures perfect fueling
Generic formulas fall short for unique needs influenced by metabolism, body type, activity levels and other factors affecting energy requirements.

Myth: All organic means completely clean
Organic labels have grey areas, as handling methods still allow certain pesticides and early picking prevents full ripening. Locally grown options provide ultimate freshness.

Myth: All vegan products are healthy

Any plant-based packaged foods heavily processed and refined deliver minimal nutrition compared to whole food sources. Check ingredients for added sugars, preservatives and isolated compounds.

Myth: Frozen produce contains maximal nutrients

Quick-freezing shortly after harvest retains some vitamins and minerals but still degrades delicate phytonutrients and plant energy lost over time.

Myth: Leftovers stay nutritious for days

While extending use of dishes for convenience, vital nutrients and beneficial compounds still slowly diminish with duration of storage as food deteriorates.

Myth: Eating globally ensures variety

Transporting produce vast distances invites early picking, irradiation, wax-coating, gassing and other cargo hold treatments - losing freshness and life force. Sourcing local in-season varieties ultimately provides peak quality.

Myth: A vegan diet lacks essential nutrients

The vegan world brims with diverse nourishing options - colorful produce, satisfying proteins and wholesome grains. Whole plant foods deliver adequate protein along with a wealth of vitamins, minerals and antioxidants for optimal health when properly sourced, combined, prepared and consumed in a holistic style.

Myth: Non-veg diet speeds up post-workout/illness/surgery recovery

All recovery capacity links directly to nutritional quality, not generic protein amounts, which plants amply supply. Further propel the recovery process by obeying innate signals as per ancient Indian wisdom, "Tongue is the doctor and Taste is the medicine."
Our inner doctor prescribes ideal medicine if we carefully listen.

The Holistic Principles of Sourcing and Using Vital Ingredients

Groceries
Favor locally grown, organic whole fruits and vegetables ripened on the vine versus conventional options with pesticide residues harvested underripe.

Grains
Choose minimally processed intact whole grains with germ and bran versus refined grains stripped of outer nutrition-protecting layers.

Honey
Select local pure, raw, unpasteurized honey retaining powerful enzymes rather than commercial filtered honey removing these.

Salt
Harvested from unpolluted seas or mineral rock deposits provide light flavor and trace minerals versus highly processed white table salt with risky additives.

Oil
Gentle expeller or cold pressing prevents damaging heat exposure preserving integrity of fatty acids as opposed to chemically extracted, solvent washed and bleached oils.

Packaged Goods
Prioritize organic, whole, minimally handled ingredients free of preservatives instead commercially prepared products listing concerning additives.

Supplements
If supplements are needed whole food based supplements supply bioavailable and bioactive forms unlike synthetic vitamins manufactured artificially in labs.

SO*ul* EASY VEGAN RECIPES

An Ideal Daily Eating Plan

I believe that an ideal eating plan should focus on sustainable living rather than following a strict short-term diet plan.

My days start by enjoying two glasses warm water first thing, then fresh lemon juice an hour later to wake up digestion. Breakfast tends to be a vibrant green juice or smoothie brimming with leafy vitality. For lunch, I indulge in a vibrant raw salad with a colourful array of vegetables dominant with leafy greens along with soaked nuts, seeds and sprouts.

Dinner keeps it light - usually steamed veggies with a small amount of cooked grains or starchy veggies like sweet potato. I try to stick to 3:1 ratio with higher veggie portions and modest carbs.

Eating this way, I stay satisfied without overloading my system. My energy smoothly rides steady all day without mean crashes or sluggishness. I feel at peace knowing my body receives what it needs when it needs while doing no harm. That inner calm extends outwards to benefit all beings!

Additionally I choose food combinations that complement each other. Beyond just eating the healthiest foods, it's so important we actually enjoy our meals with all our senses! I treat eating as a special ritual to feel gratitude and nourishment.

I pay thanks for all the efforts that brought this dish possible - from farmer to shopkeeper, from my parents to the universal energy. Then mindfully appreciate flavors, textures, colors and aromas through eyes, nose, fingers getting familiar with components before tasting.

Preparing and eating soulfully, feeds more than our physical hunger! Our souls are nourished, mind awaken and our body energised. These conscious, caring eating practices unlock nature's healing powers tremendously.

Welcome to Soul Easy Vegan Recipes.

Bringing Recipes to Life

Creating delicious recipes that nourish the body and soul brings me so much joy. And I want you, the reader, to feel that same delight with each dish you create from this book. That's why I've crafted each recipe to guide and inspire you on this plant-powered journey.

I include detailed instructions so even kitchen novices feel equipped to cook up some magic. But my goal isn't just great taste (though I promise these recipes deliver!). I also want to open your eyes to the incredible health properties hiding within ordinary fruits, veggies, grains and spices.

That's why every ingredient list highlights the key vitamins, minerals and nutrients being delivered. You'll learn how something as humble as a sweet potato or bunch of spinach holds vital compounds for fighting disease, boosting immunity and promoting longevity.

And it doesn't stop there! The nutritional and medicinal benefit sections go into greater depth on how that recipe can transform your wellbeing. I summarize the latest science and research on whole food healing in an easy-to-grasp way.

You'll also notice creative alternatives and wellness tweak suggestions in the notes of some recipes. This is where my inner alchemist likes to play! I offer guidance on adapting dishes to custom health needs, improving digestion or dialing up nutrition.

My hope is that by the end of this book, you see food as so much more than just calories to count or cravings to satisfy. These life-giving plants don't just have the ability to thrilling our tastebuds...they hold FUTURES within their cellular walls.

And those futures belong to us all when we tap into the power of eating for wellness as a daily practice.

Journey Through the Recipes

When curating the perfect alchemy of recipes for this book, I gave thoughtful attention to the flow and progression. I wanted to take you on a journey—from the simplest juices and smoothies towards heartier cooked fare and finally finishing with restorative elixirs.

RAW DETOX JUICES & SMOOTHIES

We begin with detoxifying juices and smoothies made from raw fruits and vegetables. These liquid preparations allow the body to absorb nutrients quickly without taxing the digestive fires. They supply a surge of vitamins, minerals and phytonutrients to cleanse sluggish systems.

BEVERAGES & PLANT BASED MILK

We then interlude with beverages to support digestion before exploring the rich and creamy world of plant-based milks.

SPROUTS

Next sprouts get a feature, as these living foods bridge the gap from juices to proper meals. Bursting with digestible protein and enzymes, sprouts energize cells and prime us for more solid foods ahead.

SALADS

The salad recipes highlights the endless variety this staple meal holds in a plant-based lifestyle. These raw preparations keep digestion efficient compared to cooked dishes.

SWEETS & SNACKS

Vegan Desserts recipes in this book offer a variety of recipes to suit your tastebuds without an ounce of sugar with Vegan Snacks offering the guilt-free break.

STEAMED SOUPS & VEGGIES

Soups then warm us up, offering comfort through blended vegetables and broths.

contd..

STEAMED VEGGIE PLATTERS with SAUCE or Gravy

Vegetables take centre stage next, where I explore techniques to retain nutrition when exposing plants to heat. Here is where we linger a while to showcase how marvellously vegetables translate to stunning entrées with global inspiration.

COOKED WHOLE GRAIN MEALS

Grains get their moment for those seeking heartier, more filling dishes as a plant-based protein source.

RECOVERY REMEDIES

Finally, the remedy recipes mend and restore balance, sending you off with blends designed to optimise health. We have most remedies in our kitchen and don't have to run after medicines or pharmacies or doctors. We are our best doctors when we listen to our body and mind and treat it with right environment.

This intentional sequence through raw and cooked preparations aims to not only showcase versatility in plant-based cuisine, but also educate you on crafting well-rounded, nourishing meals.

I invite you to journey through these pages and savour each recipe!

> "
>
> *kaṭv-amla-lavaṇāty-uṣhṇa- tīkṣhṇa-rūkṣa-vidāhinaḥ*
> *āhārā rājasasyeṣhṭā duḥkha-śhokāmaya-pradāḥ*
>
> **FOODS THAT ARE TOO BITTER, TOO SOUR, SALTY, VERY HOT, PUNGENT, DRY, AND FULL OF CHILLIES, ARE DEAR TO PERSONS IN THE MODE OF PASSION. SUCH FOODS PRODUCE PAIN, GRIEF, AND DISEASE.**
>
> **BHAGAVAD GITA: CHAPTER 17, VERSE 9**
>
> "

Introducing..

soul
SO EASY
VEGAN
RECIPES

The Unique Format

Introduction to Unique Recipe Format

The recipes presented in this book offer a uniquely comprehensive view of each dish. My goal is not only to provide delicious vegan meals, but to really help you understand the incredible nutritional and medicinal properties of plant-based whole foods. Here's an overview of special components you'll find with each recipe:

Ingredients Breakdown: I list out all ingredients individually, along with key vitamins, minerals, or other nutritional elements that each ingredient delivers notated in brackets. This allows you to see the wide array of macros, micronutrients, and beyond provided in natural form within plants, herbs, spices, etc. ***Please refer to page 128 for vitamins and minerals code used across this book.***

Step-by-Step Guidance: The instructions walk through preparations from start to finish in an easy-to-follow format. I aim to make cooking approachable and enjoyable, even for kitchen novices.

Nutritional Benefits: Each recipe contains a section outlining the main vitamins, minerals, fiber content, protein quality, and other nutritional elements provided in that meal. I summarize the key nutrients that support health in myriad ways.

Medicinal Benefits Section: This is a signature addition not found in typical cookbooks. I outline the key medicinal properties and research-backed health benefits of the ingredients used. My recipes aren't just delicious—they can also provide powerful healing, protective, and restorative effects for the body.

In summary, I designed these recipes not only to please your palate, but also deeply nourish your cells and transform your vitality. My integrative approach considers both flavour and function to support you on your holistic journey towards optimal wellbeing.

Keymarkers in the Recipe

Visual Representation of key ingredients

Sweet potato kale with tofu sauce

Kale leaves
(VitK, VitA, VitC, AO)
50 - 100 gms

Organic Tofu
(PB, Fe, Ca)

Nutritional Yeast
(B12, PbP, GF)

Lemon Juice
(VitC, DH)

Instructions

Wash, cut and steam the Sweet potato.

Add the washed kale leaves on top after about 10 mins.

While it gets cooked, add tofu pieces and a spoon of nutritional yeast, tablespoon of lemon juice squeezed and blend in a blender to make sauce-like consistency.

Check the softness of Sweet potato and kale and not to allow it to change the fresh green colour.

Peel the outer layer of sweet potato and arrange on a plate. Add the kale leaves and peas. Spoon in the white cheesy sauce and enjoy it as a meal on its own.

So Easy & Simple Step by Step Instructions

Tips & Remarks

Choose organic tofu as most of the soybeans are genetically modified.

PLEASE SEE PAGE 128 FOR VITAMINS & MINERALS CODES USED ACROSS THE BOOK

Each Ingredient listed with its main nutritional element like Vitamin, Minerals

Medicinal or Nutritional Benefit

Raw Detox Dinks
Smoothies &
Plant-based Milk

Lemon Ginger Vitality Drink

Ingredients:

Organic Lemon 1 *(VitC, VitB6, VitA, F)*
Organic Ginger 1 inch piece *(Mg, Zn, K)*
Optional: 1 spoon **raw honey** or an inch piece of
unprocessed jaggery
(USF, VitB6, OMG3)

Instructions:

1. Thoroughly wash the lemon and ginger to remove any foreign particles.
2. Peel the ginger skin, slice thinly, and add to a glass.
3. Cut the lemon, squeeze the juice into the glass.
4. Pour lukewarm water into the glass and stir well.
5. Optionally, add 1 spoon of raw honey or a piece of unprocessed jaggery, adjusting to taste.
6. Enjoy the drink slowly, sipping without rushing.

Note:

- Opt for seeded, organic lemon and ginger.
- Prefer unwaxed lemons for purity.
- Use only raw, unprocessed honey or jaggery.
- When using honey, best to use non-metallic spoons.

"Boosts immunity, skin health, and digestion, while aiding in detoxification, heart health, weight management, and blood sugar regulation."

Refreshing Mint Coriander Juice

Ingredients:

1 small bunch or handful of **Coriander Leaves**
(VitA, VitC, K, F)
1 small bunch or handful of **Mint Leaves**
(VitA, VitC, AO, F)
½ **Lemon** *(VitC, VitB6, VitA, F)*
1 inch **Ginger Piece** *(Mg, Zn, K)*

Instructions:

1. Thoroughly clean and chop the coriander leaves, mint leaves, lemon, and ginger.
2. Place all ingredients in a mixer.
3. Blend until smooth.
4. Enjoy your detoxifying green juice fresh and unstirred.

Note:

- Avoid adding salt to retain the natural flavours and health benefits.
- Coriander leaves can be substituted with parsley leaves or any other herbal green leaves as per your preference.

Enhances immunity and skin health with vital vitamins and antioxidants, promotes digestive wellness, and supports oral health, hydration, and anti-inflammatory benefits.

Soothing Cucumber Spinach Detox Drink

Ingredients:

Cucumber (1 to 1 & 1/2)
(VitK, VitC, P, K)
Celery Stalks *(2) (VitA, VitK, F)*
Handful of **Spinach or Beetroot**
Leaves *(VitA, VitC, Mg, Fe, Ca)*

Instructions:

1. Wash and prepare the cucumber and celery. You can
choose to grate and then squeeze through a cotton cloth or nut milk bag,
adding water to make up to a glass.
2. Alternatively, cut them into small pieces, blend in a mixer, and filter to
make a detox juice.
3. If using a slow juicer, slice the cucumber and celery into manageable
pieces and juice them along with a bunch of spinach or beetroot leaves.

Note:

- Feel free to add a dash of any green leaves you love, including ginger,
for added flavour and health benefits.
- Limit the amount of celery stalks to avoid overpowering the other
flavours.
- The remaining pulp can be used as a natural face and body mask or
added to plant compost.

Aids weight management and heart health, enhances skin and immune function with essential vitamins, and promotes blood health, digestive wellness, and anti-inflammatory benefits.

Divine Gooseberry Refreshment

Ingredients:

Gooseberries (3-4)
(VitC, VitB5, VitB6, F, AO)
Optional: **Ginger** for taste *(Mg, Zn, K)*
Optional: Bunch of **Parsley Leaves** for added chlorophyll
(VitK, VitC, VitA, F)

Instructions:

1. Wash the gooseberries thoroughly and remove the seeds.
2. Cut the gooseberries into small pieces.
3. Place them in a mixer with a sufficient amount of water. Blend until smooth.
4. Strain the mixture to obtain a clear juice.
5. Optionally, add ginger and parsley leaves during blending for additional flavour and nutrients.
6. Enjoy this miraculous drink slowly, savouring each refreshing sip.

Note:

- Ginger adds a zesty flavour and enhances the medicinal properties of the juice.
- Parsley leaves increase the chlorophyll content, further boosting the health benefits.

Boosts immunity and eye health, supports digestion and blood sugar regulation, and offers rejuvenating, anti-aging, and anti-inflammatory benefits.

Revitalising Ash Gourd Detox Drink

Ingredients:
Ash Gourd (a quarter) (VitC, K, Ca, Mg, AO)

Instructions:
1. Wash, peel, and deseed the ash gourd.
2. You can either grate the ash gourd and then squeeze the juice out using a cotton cloth or nut milk bag,
3. Or, cut it into smaller pieces, blend in a mixer, and then filter out the juice.
4. Alternatively, use a slow masticating juicer for the best nutrient retention.
5. Enjoy this rejuvenating and energising drink on its own.

Note:
- The ash gourd is renowned for its high pranic energy, making it an excellent choice for a natural energy boost.
- It is one of the best natural detoxifiers, known to help cleanse the body of toxins effectively.

Supports immune and bone health, aids in hydration and digestion, and offers cooling, detoxifying, and rejuvenating Ayurvedic benefits.

Cleansing Bottle Gourd Elixir

Ingredients:

Bottle Gourd (1) *(VitC, VitB, K, Na, Ca)*

Instructions:

1. Wash, peel, and deseed the bottle gourd.
2. Grate the bottle gourd and squeeze out the juice using a cotton cloth or nut milk bag.
3. Alternatively, cut it into smaller pieces, blend in a mixer, and then filter out the juice.
4. For optimal nutrient retention, use a slow masticating juicer.
5. Savour the cleansing drink immediately after preparation.

Note:

- Avoid using bottle gourd if it tastes bitter, as it might be harmful.
- Bottle gourd can be substituted with other vegetables from the gourd family.
- This juice, like ash gourd juice, is known for its high pranic energy and excellent detoxifying properties.

Enhances immune and bone health, supports weight management and body heat balance, and promotes kidney, liver, and overall digestive wellness.

Ginger Infused Carrot Wellness Drink

Ingredients:
Carrots (2) *(VitA, VitK, VitB6, F, AO)*
Ginger (1 inch size) *(Mg, Zn, K)*

Instructions:
1. Wash the carrots and ginger thoroughly, snipping off the ends.
2. Grate the ingredients and squeeze out the juice using a cotton cloth, muslin cloth, or nut milk bag.
3. Alternatively, chop into smaller pieces, blend, and then strain the juice.
4. For maximum nutrient preservation, use a slow masticating juicer.
5. Enjoy this rejuvenating and energising drink on its own.

Note:
- Carrots yield less juice compared to other fruits and vegetables; add water as needed to adjust the volume.
- Retain the outer layer of the carrot during preparation to preserve essential minerals, vitamins, and phytonutrients.

Boosts vision and immune health, enhances skin and digestive wellness, and supports cardiovascular function with anti-inflammatory benefits.

Immune Boosting Beet Juice

Ingredients:

Beetroots (2) *(F, VitC, VitB9, Mg, Iron)*
Ginger (1 inch size) *(Mg, Zn, K)*

Instructions:

1. Thoroughly wash and peel the beetroots and ginger.
2. Grate the ingredients and squeeze out the juice using a cotton cloth, muslin cloth, or nut milk bag.
3. Alternatively, chop into smaller pieces, blend, and then strain the juice.
4. For optimal nutrient retention, use a slow masticating juicer.
5. Enjoy this rejuvenating and energising drink on its own.

Note:

- Beetroot juice yields less juice than other vegetables; add water as needed to adjust the volume.
- Adding carrots can enhance the taste while balancing the natural sugars.
- Enjoy beet and carrot juice in moderation to avoid excessive sugar intake. Savour it slowly, sip by sip.

Enhances digestive health and immunity, supports heart and liver function, and offers stamina, detoxification, and anti-inflammatory benefits

Refreshing Tomato Pepper Fusion

Ingredients:

Tomatoes (2) *(VitC, VitK, VitA, Lycopene)*
Red Pepper (1) *(VitC, VitB6, AO)*
Cucumber (1/2) *(VitK, VitC, P, K)*
Coriander Leaves (Bunch) *(VitA, VitC, K, F)*
Lemon (1/2) *(VitC, VitB6, VitA, F)*

Instructions:

1. Wash, deseed, and cut the tomatoes and red pepper.
2. Add the chopped cucumber slices and coriander leaves to a slow juicer.
3. Pour the mixture into a glass.
4. Squeeze in the juice of ½ a lemon for added flavour.
5. Enjoy this purifying detox juice fresh.
6. If not having the slow juicer, slice the ingredients and juice them in the mixer and filter it.

Note:

- Feel free to enhance the flavour with green leaves or ginger.
- Use the remaining pulp as a natural face and body mask, or add it to plant compost.
- Due to the acidity of tomatoes, consume this juice in moderation.
- Always use fully ripened tomatoes.

Boosts immunity and skin health, supports heart and liver function, aids in detoxification, and helps maintain healthy blood pressure with hydrating and antioxidant-rich ingredients

Nature's Hydration Miracle

Ingredients:
Fresh Tender Coconut (1) *(USF, Manganese, F)*

Instructions:
1. Carefully slit open the top part of the fresh tender coconut.
2. Insert a steel or paper straw and enjoy the coconut water immediately for the best taste and nutrient retention.
3. Consume it as soon as it's cut to experience its full benefits.

Note:
- If purchasing from a vendor, ensure the coconut is only partially opened and not fully exposed or bottled.
- Living in a region with access to fresh tender coconuts, incorporate it regularly into your diet to reap its full health benefits.
- Packaged coconut water, due to processing for shelf life, does not offer the same health benefits as fresh coconut water.

Enhances hydration and heart health, supports weight management and electrolyte balance, and offers digestive, anti-inflammatory, and rejuvenating benefits.

Green Power Morning Smoothie

Ingredients:

Spinach Leaves (50 gms or 2 handfuls) *(VitA, VitC, VitK, Mg, Fe)*
Natural Dates (2-3) *(F, VitB5, VitB6, K)*
Apple (1) *(VitC, VitB6, F, AO)*
Ginger Piece (1 inch) *(Mg, Zn, K)*

Instructions:

1. Wash the spinach leaves, dates, apple, and ginger thoroughly.
2. Add all the ingredients to a blender.
3. Blend until smooth.
4. Enjoy the smoothie immediately for maximum freshness and nutrient benefit.

Note:

- The addition of fruits like apples or bananas makes the smoothie tastier and more appealing, especially during the initial transition to a natural lifestyle.
- You can substitute the apple with a banana for a sweeter, more filling smoothie, ideal as a quick breakfast option.
- Gradually aim to include more leafy greens and vegetables in your smoothies for enhanced health benefits.

Promotes eye, immune, and bone health, enhances digestion and energy, and supports heart health and natural dietary transition with nutrient-rich ingredients.

Nutty Protein Power Bowl

Ingredients:

Soaked Walnuts (4) (PbP, OMG3, VitE)
Soaked and Peeled Almonds (4-6)
(PbP, VitE, Mg, Ca)
Soaked Pumpkin Seeds *1 tablespoon (PbP, Mg, Zn, K)*
Natural Dates (4) *(F, VitB5, VitB6, K)*
Moong Bean Sprouts (1 handful) *(PbP, VitC, F, K)*
Toppings: **Fresh Coconut Flakes** *(USF, F, Manganese)* and **Soaked Chia Seeds** *(PbP, OMG3, F)*
Collard Greens (1 handful) *(VitA, VitC, VitK, Ca)*

Instructions:

1. Wash the collard greens, dates, and moong bean sprouts thoroughly.
2. Add the soaked walnuts, almonds, pumpkin seeds, dates, sprouts, and collard greens to a blender.
3. Blend with some coconut water until smooth.
4. Serve in a bowl, topping with fresh coconut flakes and soaked chia seeds.

Boosts muscle repair and heart health, supports bone strength and digestive wellness, and enhances overall vitality with rich plant-based proteins and omega-3s.

Note:

- Feel free to swap collard greens with other leafy vegetables according to your taste and the season.
- This protein-rich smoothie is ideal for post-workout recovery or as a fulfilling breakfast option.

Energising Green Sprout Delight

Ingredients:

Mung Sprouts (Handful) *(PbP, VitC, F, K)*
Fresh Coconut (½ Cup) *(USF, F, Manganese)*
Coriander Leaves (A Bunch) *(VitA, VitC, K, F)*
Optional: **Dates for taste** *(Fiber, VitB5, VitB6, K)*
Toppings: Soaked **Sesame Seeds** and **Sunflower Seeds**

Instructions:

1. Wash the mung sprouts and coriander leaves thoroughly.
2. Add the sprouts, fresh coconut kernels or flakes, and optional dates to a blender.
3. Blend with the coconut water obtained from the fresh coconut until smooth.
4. Enjoy the smoothie with a topping of soaked sesame seeds and sunflower seeds.

Note:

- This smoothie is a great way to incorporate sprouts into your diet, known for their high nutritional value and digestibility.
- The addition of dates adds natural sweetness, making it more palatable for those new to green smoothies.

Enhances muscle growth and digestive health, supports heart and immune function, and boosts energy and wellness with rich plant proteins and healthy fats.

Sweet Indulgence Banana Date Smoothie

Ingredients:

Banana (1) *(VitB6, VitC, Potassium, F)*
Dates (4) *(fiber, VitB5, VitB6, K)*

Instructions:

1. Peel the banana and remove the seeds from the dates. Wash them thoroughly.
2. Add the banana and dates to a blender with a sufficient amount of water or you could replace the water with plant-based milk for a more creamy outcome.
3. Blend until smooth and creamy.
4. For an extra rich and creamy treat, add a little coconut milk to the blend.
5. Enjoy this tasty smoothie slowly, savouring each sip.

Note:

- Remember that fruits are best consumed whole, as juicing or blending can lead to a loss of some nutrients and result in concentrated sugar intake.
- Enjoy this smoothie occasionally as a healthier alternative to processed sweet treats.
- You can add blueberries or other sweet fruits like figs for variety. However, avoid mixing acidic and sweet fruits

Boosts heart and digestive health, provides quick energy and natural sweetness, and contributes to a balanced, enjoyable diet with vitamins and healthy fats.

Green Bliss Kale Coconut Bowl

Ingredients:

Kale Leaves (Bunch) *(VitA, VitC, VitK, Ca)*
Fresh Coconut (½ Cup) *(USF, F, Manganese)*
Dates (4) *(F, VitB5, VitB6, K)*
Soaked **Pumpkin Seeds** and **Pecan Nuts** 1tbsp

Instructions:

1. Thoroughly wash the kale leaves and deseed the dates.
2. Combine the kale, dates, and coconut in a blender with water.
3. Blend until smooth.
4. Pour the smoothie into a bowl and top with soaked pumpkin seeds and pecan nuts.

Note:

- For an extra tasty treat, add a banana and 4 tablespoons of Brazil nut milk to the blend.
- This smoothie bowl is a great way to incorporate kale, a superfood, into your diet.
- The addition of nuts and seeds adds a crunchy texture and additional nutrients.

Enhances immune, vision, and bone health, supports heart and brain function, and boosts energy and wellness with nutrient-rich greens, nuts, and seeds

Warm Beverages & Plant-based Milk

Welcome to the world of aromatic spices like cinnamon, cardamom and ginger paired with the creaminess of almonds, oats and millet.

These drinks are simple, healthy and remind us that plant-powered diets need not lack in flavour or luxury!

I can already imagine the smile these special beverages will bring as you wrap your cold fingers around a steamy mug.

Soothing Cardamom Ginger Herbal Tea

Ingredients:

Curry Leaves (a small bunch) *(VitA, VitC, VitB, Ca, Iron)*
Cardamom (2-3) *(Mg, Zn, Ca, VitC)*
Ginger (1 inch, sliced) *(Mg, Zn, K)*
Optional: **Jaggery** for taste *(Iron, Mg, Potassium)*

Instructions:

1. Pour 1 glass of water into a vessel and heat it on a low flame.
2. Add the curry leaves, sliced ginger, and cardamom to the water.
3. Let it simmer until you notice a delightful aroma emanating from the infusion.
4. You can choose to drink it as is or add a small piece of unrefined jaggery for added sweetness.
5. Filter the tea and enjoy this soothing beverage.

Note:

- Curry leaves can be substituted with fresh coriander leaves, mint leaves, natural dried rose petals, or fruit peelings like orange rind and pomegranate skin for variety.
- For a creamier and richer flavour, consider adding homemade almond milk or Brazil nut milk to the tea.

Supports digestion and stress relief, offers anti-inflammatory and antioxidant benefits, and provides a caffeine-free energy boost with natural sweetness and unique flavours.

Spiced Aromatic Masala Tea

Ingredients:

Cinnamon Stick *(Mg, Ca, Iron, AO)*
Cloves *(Manganese, VitK, Mg, AO)*
Fennel Seeds (Saunf) *(VitC, Ca, Iron, Mg)*
Cardamom *(Mg, Zn, Ca, VitC)*
Black Peppercorns *(K, VitA, VitC, AO)*
Ginger or Dry Ginger Powder *(Mg, Zn, K)*
Optional: **Unrefined Jaggery** for taste *(Iron, Mg, Potassium)*

Instructions:

1. Add water to a pan and heat it on a low flame.
2. Add (according to the taste) the cinnamon stick, cloves, fennel seeds, cardamom, black peppercorns, and ginger or dry ginger powder to the water.
3. Allow the mixture to simmer until you can smell the fragrant aroma of the spices.
4. If desired, add unrefined jaggery for a touch of sweetness. Stir well.
5. Filter the tea and serve hot.

> Enhances digestion and nutrient absorption, offers warming and soothing benefits, boosts immunity, and provides a natural energy boost with healthful spices and jaggery.

Note:

- You can enhance the flavour of the tea by adding dried rose petals or other dried herbal flowers.
- This masala tea is versatile and can be customised with different spices and herbal additions according to personal preference and taste.

Warm Cinnamon Turmeric Comfort

Ingredients:

Cinnamon Stick or Powder
(1 pinch without preservatives) *(Mg, Ca, Iron, AO)*
Turmeric Powder (1 pinch) *(Curcumin, Mg, VitC, K)*
Almond Milk or **Brazil Nut Milk** (1 cup) *(VitE, Mg, Ca, PbP)*

Instructions:

1. Warm a cup of your preferred nut milk (almond or Brazil nut) slightly.
2. Add a pinch each of cinnamon powder and turmeric powder to the warm milk.
3. Stir well to combine the ingredients evenly.
4. Enjoy this warm and comforting drink for a relaxing evening.

Note:

- This tea is an excellent choice for winding down after a busy day, with its soothing spices and warm nut milk.
- Cinnamon and turmeric are both renowned for their anti-inflammatory and antioxidant properties, making this tea not only comforting but also beneficial for health.

Supports heart health and digestion, reduces inflammation, boosts brain function and immunity, with antioxidant-rich spices and nutritious nut milk.

Revitalising Finger Millet Beverage

Ingredients:

Finger Millet Powder (2 tablespoons)
(PbP, Calcium, Iron, Dietary fiber)

Instructions:

1. Boil 2 cups of water in a vessel.
2. In a small bowl, mix 2 tablespoons of ragi (finger millet) flour with a little water to form a lump-free paste.
3. Gradually add this mixture to the boiling water, stirring continuously to prevent lumps.
4. Cook until you notice a pleasant aroma of cooked finger millet, then turn off the heat.
5. Let the drink cool slightly. It can be consumed warm with a bit of salt to taste as a drink, or you can make it thicker to enjoy like porridge.
6. Pair it with steamed vegetables for a protein-rich meal.

Note:

- For a variation, especially for children, a little bit of any plant-based milk can be added for extra flavour.

Boosts heart and digestive health, provides quick energy and natural sweetness, and contributes to a balanced, enjoyable diet with vitamins and healthy fats.

Luxurious Saffron Infused Almond Treat

Ingredients:

Almond Milk (1 cup) *(VitE, Mg, Ca, PbP)*
Saffron Strands (A Pinch)
(Manganese, VitC, Potassium)
Optional: **Dates Paste** or **Unrefined Jaggery** for taste
(Iron, Mg, Potassium)

Instructions:

1. Warm the almond milk with a little water to adjust the consistency to your liking.
2. Stir in dates paste or unrefined jaggery for a natural sweetness.
3. Sprinkle a pinch of saffron strands into the warm milk.
4. Enjoy this comforting and aromatic beverage warm.

Note:

- Use saffron sparingly, as too much can cause heat in the body.
- This drink is a delightful way to experience the unique flavours and health benefits of saffron in a soothing almond milk base.

Promotes skin and bone health, enhances mood and heart function, and offers a nourishing, calming beverage for evening relaxation with vitamin-rich almond milk and saffron.

Homemade Nutrient Rich Milk Alternatives

Almond Milk

Ingredients: 1 Cup Almonds *(VitE, Mg, Ca, PbP)*
Instructions: Soak 1 cup of almonds overnight. Blend with 1 cup of water and strain using a nut milk bag or white cotton sieve cloth.
Add more water, squeeze again, and store in a glass jar in the fridge. *Use within 2-3 days.*

Brazil Nut Milk

Ingredients: 1 Cup Brazil Nuts *(Se, Mg, Ca, PbP)*
Instructions: Follow the same process as for almond milk. Soak Brazil nuts overnight, blend, strain, and store in the fridge. Use within 2-3 days.

Coconut Milk

Ingredients: 1 Fresh Coconut *(USF, Manganese, F)*
Instructions: Break open the coconut and slice it into thin pieces. Blend with 1 cup of water, strain, and repeat with more water. Use immediately for best taste or store in the fridge for up to 2 days.

Oat Milk

Ingredients: 1 Cup Whole Rolled Oats *(VitB, F, Mg, Iron)*
Instructions: Soak 1 cup of oats overnight. Wash, blend with 1 cup water, and strain. Add more water, squeeze again. Suitable for drinks or creamy puddings. Store in the fridge.

Supports bone health and digestion, provides plant-based proteins and healthy fats, and is ideal for lactose intolerance with heart-healthy, blood sugar-regulating properties.

Raw Sprouts & Salads

Homegrown Mung Bean Sprouts

Ingredients:

Mung beans (1 cup) *(PbP, VitC, F)*

Instructions:

1. Wash and soak the mung beans overnight.

2. Rinse the soaked beans and tie them in a white cotton cloth.

3. Place the cloth in a bowl, cover it with a lid, and store in a warm place.

4. Allow 24 to 48 hours for sprouting, until white sprouts shoot out of the cotton cloth.

5. Enjoy the sprouts as a snack, with soaked nuts or seeds, or in a salad.

Note:

- Use the sprouts before the white tail turns brown to ensure freshness.

- Sprouting in a cloth is usually easier and faster compared to using glass bottles.

- The sprouting duration may vary slightly depending on the outside temperature. Soaking in warm water fasten the sprouting process.

- Mung bean sprouts are an excellent source of digestible protein and nutrients.

Boosts muscle repair and immune function, supports heart health and digestion, and offers antioxidant, anti-inflammatory, and dietary balance benefits, ideal for weight management.

Nutritious Fenugreek Sprouting at Home

Ingredients:

Fenugreek Seeds (1 tbsp)

(F, Iron, Mg, VitC)

Instructions:

1. Wash and soak the fenugreek seeds overnight.
2. Rinse the soaked seeds and tie them in a white cotton cloth.
3. Place the cloth in a bowl, cover with a lid, and store in a warm place.
4. Allow 24 to 48 hours for sprouting, until white sprouts of about 1 inch or more appear.
5. Enjoy the sprouts as a nutritious snack, with soaked nuts or seeds, or in salads.

Note:

- Harvest the sprouts before the white tail turns brown to ensure optimal freshness and nutritional value.
- Sprouting duration can vary slightly depending on the outside temperature.
- Fenugreek sprouts tend to grow faster than other sprouts and are known for their health benefits, especially in managing diabetes.

Enhances digestion and immune health, supports blood sugar regulation and heart health, and offers anti-inflammatory benefits, ideal for maintaining overall well-being

Crunchy Raw Veggie Medley

Ingredients:

Carrots *(VitA, VitK, F)* - 1
Coconut Kernels *(MCTs, Manganese)* - 3-4
Cabbage *(VitC, VitK, fibre)* - Small Slice
Cilantro *(VitA, VitC, Iron)* - 1 Bunch
Pine Nuts *(PbP, VitE, Mg)* - 1 tbsp
Pumpkin Seeds *(PbP, Mg, Zn)* - 1 tbsp
Optional: **Sesame Seed Sauce** *(Ca, Mg, VitE)*

Instructions:

1. Wash all vegetables thoroughly under running water.

2. Grate carrots and thinly slice cabbage into bite-size pieces. Roughly chop cilantro.

3. In a salad bowl, arrange the grated carrots, cabbage slices and cilantro. Top with coconut kernels and soaked nuts and seeds.

4. Add sesame seed sauce before serving for extra flavour (optional).

Note:

- Use seasonal veggies and swap ingredients to suit your taste.
- Cut pieces larger to preserve nutrients.

Enhances immunity, digestion, and heart health, offers nutrient-rich, low-calorie nourishment, and provides anti-inflammatory and antioxidant benefits.

Asian Inspired Salad Topper

Ingredients:

Soaked Sesame Seeds *(Ca, Mg, VitE)* - ¼ Cup
Dates, Pitted *(F, K)* - 4
Lemon *(VitC)* - ½
Coconut Meat *(MCTs, Manganese)* - 2 Pieces
Black Pepper *(VitK)* - to taste
Optional: **Pine Nuts** *(PbP, VitE, Mg)*

Instructions:

1. Soak sesame seeds overnight.
2. Add soaked seeds, pitted dates, lemon, coconut meat and peppercorns into a blender. Blend into a coarse powder.
3. Slowly add 2-3 tbsp water while blending to reach a smooth, pourable consistency.
4. Stir in pine nuts (optional).
5. Drizzle sesame sauce over salads or enjoy as a dip.

Note:

Still tasty without nuts, if you want to avoid nuts.

Delivers essential nutrients with fibre, protein, and vitamins, boosts bone and dental health, and offers anti-inflammatory and alkalizing benefits.

Chilled Garden Crunch

Ingredients:

Cucumber *(VitK, Manganese)* - 1/2
Red Bell Pepper *(VitC, VitA)* - 1/2
Celery *(Folate, Potassium)* - 1 Stalk
Cherry Tomatoes *(Lycopene, VitC)* - 4-5
Basil Leaves *(VitK, Iron)* - 1 Bunch
Optional Toppings:
Pumpkin Seeds *(PbP, Mg, Zn)* - 1tsp
Pine Nuts *(PbP, VitE, Mg)*- 1tsp

Instructions:

1. Wash all vegetables thoroughly. Slice cucumber, bell pepper, celery and tomato.

2. On a platter or in a salad bowl, arrange sliced veggies. Top with basil leaves.

3. Sprinkle on soaked pumpkin seeds and pine nuts before serving (optional).

4. Drizzle with Basil Leaf Green Chutney.

Note:

Use seasonal vegetables and tailor ingredients to your tastes.

Boosts heart, liver, and immune health, offers nutrient-rich, low-calorie nourishment with antioxidants, and aids in digestion and gut health.

Beet Parsnip Salad with Tofu Sauce

Ingredients:

Beetroot (1) (VitC, Folate, F)
Parsnip (1) (VitC, F, Potassium)
Fresh Green Peas (VitC, VitK, Manganese, F)
Leafy Savoy Cabbage (2 Big Leaves) (VitK, VitC, Folate)
Soaked Walnuts (Omega-3 Fatty Acids, Protein)
Chia Seeds (Fibre, Protein, Omega-3 Fatty Acids)
Tofu (PbP, Calcium, Iron)
Lemon Juice (VitC, VitB6)
Sesame Seeds Paste (Calcium, Protein)

Instructions:

1. Wash, cut, and place beetroot, parsnip, and green peas. Cut into thin finger-sized sticks.
2. Arrange the veggies on a savoy cabbage leaf.
3. Top the salad with the tofu sauce, soaked walnuts, and chia seeds.

> Boosts overall health with rich vitamins and antioxidants, supports heart health and digestion, and enhances plant-based protein intake with a creamy, low-calorie tofu sauce

Quick Tofu Sauce Recipe

Ingredients: Organic Tofu, Lemon Juice, Nutritional Yeast - 1tsp
Instructions: Blend tofu in a blender along with lemon juice and nutritional yeast to create a cheesy and nutty sauce.

Rainbow Garden Salad with Sprouts

Ingredients:

Mung Bean Sprouts *(PbP, VitC, F)* - Handful
Carrots *(VitA, VitK)* - 1
Red Bell Pepper *(VitC, VitA)* - 1
Green Cabbage *(VitK, F)* - 1-2 Leaves
Coconut Kernels *(MCTs, Manganese)* - 2 Pieces
Sesame Seeds *(Ca, Mg, Iron)* - 2 Tbsp
Dates *(Potassium, F)* - 2
Macadamia Nuts *(PbP, VitE, Mg)* - 4-6
Lemon Juice *(VitC)* - 1 Tbsp
Optional: **Sesame Chutney**

Instructions:

1. Rinse sprouts and pat dry thoroughly. Wash, peel, and slice other vegetables.
2. In a salad bowl, layer sprouts, carrots, pepper, cabbage and coconut kernels.
3. Top with soaked sesame seeds, chopped dates and macadamia nuts.
4. Finish with lemon juice. Add sesame date chutney if desired.

Note:

Enjoy sprouts when white tips have grown to 1-11/2 inches for maximum nutrition.
Enjoy cut vegetables within 15 minutes to avoid further oxidation.

Boosts muscle repair and immune function, supports heart health and digestion, and offers antioxidant, anti-inflammatory, and dietary balance benefits, ideal for weight management.

Ginger Lime Cilantro Drizzle

Ingredients:

Cilantro Leaves *(VitA, VitC)* - 1 Small Bunch
Coconut Kernels *(MCTs, Manganese)* - 2 Pieces
Ginger Root *(VitC, Magnesium)* - 1 Inch Piece
Black Peppercorns *(VitK, Manganese)* - 5-6
Lemon Juice *(Vitamin C)* - 1 Tbsp
Optional: **Dates** *(F, Potassium)* - 2

Instructions:

1. Wash cilantro leaves. Add to the blender.
2. Add coconut kernels, ginger, peppercorns and ¼ cup water. Blend into a slightly coarse mixture.
3. Squeeze in lemon juice and give it a tangy twist. Add pitted dates for sweetness if desired.
4. Transfer chutney to an air-tight jar. Spoon over sprout salads.

Note:

Delicious when paired with sprouts, salads or Dosas too.

Enhances digestive and gut health, offers high-nutrient, low-calorie benefits with vitamins and anti-inflammatory properties, and provides antibacterial effects through potent herbs.

Courgette Ribbons with Basil Pesto

Ingredients:

Zucchini *(VitC, Manganese)* - 1
Cherry Tomatoes *(Lycopene, VitC)* - 10
Yellow Bell Pepper *(VitC, VitA)* - 1
Basil Leaves *(VitK, VitA)* - 1 Bunch
Dates, Pitted *(F, Potassium)* - 3
Pine Nuts *(PbP, VitE, Mg)* - 2 Tbsp
Optional: **Cracked Black Pepper, Pink Salt**

Instructions:

1. Wash all produce. Slice zucchini and bell pepper into long strips with a spiralizer or vegetable peeler to create noodles.
2. In a small blender or food processor, combine basil, dates and pine nuts along with cherry tomatoes. Blend/process into a textured pesto, adding water only if needed.
3. In a large bowl, mix the zucchini and pepper noodles, cherry tomatoes and prepared pesto. Toss well until coated.
4. Top with cracked black pepper and pink salt before serving (optional).

Note:

Choose Organic Red Peppers instead of other colours as they are genetically modified.

Boosts immunity, aids in digestion, and promotes heart, skin, and eye health, with low-calorie, high-antioxidant ingredients for detoxifying effects

Crunchy Cauli Courgette Sandwich

Ingredients:

Zucchini *(VitC, Manganese)* - 1
Fenugreek Sprouts *(F, VitC)* - 2 Tbsp
Grated Cauliflower Florets *(VitC, Folate)* - 3-4
Cauliflower Leaves *(VitK)* - 5-6
Cilantro Leaves *(VitA)* - 1 Bunch
Mint Leaves *(VitA)* - Handful
Lemon Juice *(VitC)* - 1 Tbsp
Gooseberry *(VitC)* - 1
Green Bell Pepper *(VitC, VitA)* - 1
Black Peppercorns *(VitK) - half tsp*

Instructions:

1. Wash all ingredients. Make chutney by blending cauliflower leaves, herbs, lemon, gooseberry and peppercorns.
2. Slice zucchini lengthwise. Gently spread open.
3. Layer fenugreek sprouts and grated cauliflower florets onto bottom zucchini slice.
4. Spoon chutney over.
5. Slice sandwich and serve.

Enhances liver and immune health, offers cell protection and repair, and provides rich antioxidants and nutrients for detoxification and hormonal balance.

Note:

Always choose organic cauliflower when possible. Minimise intake initially if thyroid issues present. Optionally soaked nuts can be added in chutney.

Veggie Stuffed Savoy Cabbage Wraps

Ingredients:

Cauliflower (¼ portion) *(VitC, VitK, F, AO)*
Beetroot (1) *(F, VitC, Iron, Mg)*
Savoy Cabbage Leaves (2) *(VitK, VitC, VitA, F)*
Red Capsicum/Bell Pepper *(VitC, VitA, AO)*
Cucumber (½) *(VitK, VitC, P, K)*
French Beans (4-5) *(VitA, VitC, F, Iron)*
Carrot (1) *(VitA, VitK, VitB6, F)*
Parsnip (½ for chutney) *(F, VitC, VitK, Manganese)*
Cauliflower Leaves handful (VitC, VitK, F, AO)

Instructions:

1. Grate the cauliflower and beetroot.

2. Slit the red capsicum and cucumber into thin, finger-size vertical slices.

3. Trim the tails of the French beans and carrot, cutting them lengthwise into the desired shape.

4. To make the cauliflower leaf chutney, grind cauliflower leaves with parsnip, adding gooseberry, pepper, and lemon juice for flavour.

5. Wash the savoy cabbage leaves and use them as a bowl or wrap.

6. Add the grated cauliflower, sliced capsicum, cucumber, beans, carrot, and top with cauliflower leaf chutney.

7. Roll with another leaf to make a wrap, or cover with another leaf to eat as a complete meal.

Boosts immune and heart health, supports digestion with high fibre, and offers a nutrient-rich, low-calorie meal with anti-inflammatory benefits

Zesty Chard Rolls with Beet Chutney

Ingredients:

Beetroot Leaves (4-5) *(VitC, VitA, F, Iron)*

Peppercorns (5-6) *(K, VitA, VitC, AO)*

Ginger (1 inch slice) *(Mg, Zn, K)*

Fennel Seeds (1 teaspoon) *(VitC, Ca, Iron, Mg)*

Coconut or Soaked Sunflower Seeds *(PbP, VitE, Mg, USF)*

Chard Leaves *(VitA, VitC, VitK, Mg)*

Celery Stalks (2) *(VitA, VitK, F, K)*

Cucumber (1) *(VitK, VitC, P, K)*

Jalapeños (as per taste) *(VitC, VitA, Capsaicin)*

Unsalted Olives (3-4) *(VitE, Iron, Copper)*

Instructions:

1. Blend beetroot leaves with stalks, soaked sunflower seeds or coconut, peppercorns, ginger, and fennel seeds to make a puree.

2. Lay out the chard leaves on a plate.

3. Cut and add celery stalks, cucumber, jalapeno bits, and spoon in the beet leaf chutney. Add soaked sunflower seeds and olives.

4. Roll them up to create spring rolls.

> Enhances immune and bone health with vitamin-rich greens, supports digestive health and provides anti-inflammatory and metabolism-boosting benefits in a nutrient-dense meal.

Note:

- Younger leaves are recommended for their tenderness in raw salads.

- Squeeze lemon for an added tangy taste if desired.

Crisp Radish Romaine Delight & Nutty Sauce

Ingredients:

Small Red Radish (6-7) *(VitC, F, K, Iron)*
Celery Stalk (1) *(VitA, VitK, F, K)*
Cucumber (½) *(VitK, VitC, P, K)*
Capsicum (½) *(VitC, VitA, AO)*
Romaine Leaves handful *(VitA, VitK, VitC, Folate)*
Soaked Pumpkin Seeds (1 tablespoon) *(PbP, Mg, Zn, K)*

For Nutty Sauce Dressing:
Soaked Raw Cashews *(⅓ cup) (PbP, Mg, VitK, Iron)*
Soaked Raw Peanuts *(PbP, VitE, Biotin, Mg)*
Fresh Dill *(VitC, VitA, Ca, Iron)*
Lemon Juice *(2 tablespoons) (VitC, VitB6, F)*
Homemade Almond Milk *(¼ cup or 2-3 tablespoons) (VitE, Mg, Ca, PbP)*
Pepper *for taste*

contd..

Crisp Radish Romaine Delight & Nutty Sauce

Instructions:

1. Thinly slice the small red radishes, celery stalk, cucumber, and capsicum.

2. Toss the vegetables in a bowl and sprinkle with soaked pumpkin seeds.

3. For the nutty sauce dressing, blend the soaked raw cashews or peanuts, fresh dill, lemon juice, and homemade almond milk until smooth. Season with pepper to taste.

4. Drizzle the creamy dill nutty sauce dressing over the salad just before serving.

Note:

- This salad combines the crispness of fresh vegetables with the creaminess of a homemade nutty sauce dressing, making it a perfect side dish or light meal.
- Avoid cashew and peanuts (because of toxins) and swap with other nuts like brazil, almond, peacan or pine nuts.

Enhances immune and skin health with vitamin C, supports weight management with low-calorie ingredients, and offers heart and brain benefits from omega-3 fatty acids in a nutrient-rich, hydrating salad.

Fresh Bok Choy Salad with Sprouts and Nuts

Ingredients:

Bok Choy Leaves (3-4) *(VitA, VitC, VitK, Ca)*
Baby Corns (4-5) *(VitB, F, C, P)*
Sprouts of Your Choice *(PbP, VitC, F, K)*
Soaked Brazil Nuts (5-6) *(Se, Mg, PbP, VitE)*
Hemp Seeds (2 tablespoons) *(PbP, OMG3, OMG6, VitE)*
Lemon Juice *(VitC, VitB6, F)*

Instructions:

1. Arrange washed bok choy leaves on a plate, resembling a tree for visual appeal.
2. Add your choice of sprouts, such as mung bean or fenugreek, along with baby corn and choice of water-rich vegetables.
3. Top the salad with soaked brazil nuts and hemp seeds.
4. Drizzle with lemon juice for a refreshing zest.

Note:

Any nut-based or parsnip based chutney can be used to add variety and flavour.

Enhances immune and bone health with vitamins A, C, K, supports thyroid and heart function with selenium and omega fatty acids, and offers anti-inflammatory benefits in an antioxidant-rich meal.

Vibrant Cabbage Roll with Nutty Sauce

Ingredients:

Grated Carrot (1) *(VitA, VitK, VitB6, F)*

Purple Cabbage (¼) *(VitC, VitK, VitA, F)*

Fresh Green Peas (A Handful) *(PbP, VitC, VitK, F)*

Soaked Peanuts (6-7) *(PbP, VitE, Biotin, Mg)*

Lemon Juice *(VitC, VitB6, F)*

Nutritional Yeast (1 tablespoon) *(B Vitamins, PbP, Zn)*

Instructions:

1. Blend the overnight soaked peanuts with nutritional yeast and lemon juice until it is smooth and creamy.

2. Wash the outer leaves of the purple cabbage to use as a wrap and grate or slice the remaining cabbage into thin strips.

3. Grate 1 carrot.

4. Place a cabbage leaf on a plate, and add the grated or sliced cabbage, carrot, and green peas.

5. Drizzle with the peanut sauce, roll it up, and enjoy as a wrap.

Boosts immune and vision health with vitamins, supports heart function and energy levels with protein, and aids in digestion and stress reduction in a nutritious wrap.

Note:

Choose organic peanuts but better to minimise them and can be swapped with pine nuts or parsnips for variety.

Sweets & Snacks

Luscious Avocado Pudding with Coconut

Ingredients

Avocado (1)
(VitE, VitK, Potassium, USF)

Coconut Kernels (5-6)
(USF, F, Manganese)

Dates (4)
(F, VitB5, VitB6, K)

Indulge in the creamy luxury of this avocado and coconut pudding, a delightful fusion of rich textures and natural sweetness

Instructions

1. Wash the avocado, cut it open, and remove the seed.
2. Spoon out the avocado flesh and place it in a blender.
3. Add chopped fresh coconut kernels and stoned dates to the blender.
4. Blend until smooth and creamy.
5. Transfer the mixture to a bowl, and sprinkle with fresh coconut gratings and dates for garnish.

Notes

This pudding is a simple, yet luxurious treat that combines the richness of avocado with the sweetness of coconut and dates.

Enhances heart health and skin vitality with healthy fats and vitamins, supports digestion and bone health, and offers brain health benefits in a nutrient-rich, indulgent dessert

Saffron Infused Chia Delicacy

Ingredients

Chia Seeds (2 tablespoons)
(PbP, OMG3, F, Ca)

Homemade Almond Milk or Brazil Nut Milk (As per required creaminess)
(VitE, Mg, Ca, PbP)

Saffron Strands (4-5)
(Manganese, VitC, Potassium)

Instructions

1. Place the overnight soaked chia seeds in a dessert bowl.
2. Add your choice of plant-based milk (almond or Brazil nut milk) to achieve the desired creaminess.
3. Sprinkle with saffron strands for flavour and garnish.

"Relish the simple elegance of this chia seed pudding, infused with saffron for a touch of luxury in your wholesome routine."

Notes

- For added sweetness and flavour, consider adding sliced dates or unrefined palm jaggery.
- This pudding is not only a delight to the palate but also packed with nutrition.

Supports bone and brain health, aids digestion, boosts mood, and provides essential nutrients for a healthy energy-sustaining snack.

Homemade Vanilla Bliss Ice Cream

Ingredients

Pure Vanilla Extract
(1 tablespoon) (Natural Flavour)
Coconut Milk (1 cup)
(USF, F, Manganese)
Soaked Cashews (10-15) *(PbP, Mg, VitK, Iron)*
Dates (4)
(F, VitB5, VitB6, K)
Fully Ripened Bananas (4)
(VitB6, VitC, Potassium, F)

Instructions

1. Peel and cut the bananas into small pieces, place them in a box, and freeze for 4-5 hours. Soak the cashews in water during this time.
2. Remove the bananas from the freezer.
3. Blend the soaked cashews and dates into a paste in a blender.
4. Add 1 cup of coconut milk and the frozen bananas, blending until creamy.
5. Pour the mixture into a glass container and freeze overnight.
6. Scoop out and enjoy the soft, creamy ice cream.
7. Garnish with date bits and soaked nuts for added texture and flavour.

Relish the simple pleasure of homemade vanilla ice cream. (those with nut allergies can use Maca powder instead of Cashews)

Offers heart-healthy fats, essential vitamins, and fibre for digestive health, energy, and muscle function in a vegan-friendly dessert.

Sesame Seed Power Balls

Ingredients

Unhulled Sesame Seeds (1 cup)
(Ca, Mg, Zn, PbP)

Unrefined Jaggery (½ cup)
(Iron, Mg, Potassium)

Notes

Black sesame seeds are often considered more nutritious than white sesame seeds, offering a higher concentration of certain nutrients.

Instructions

1. Dry roast the sesame seeds in a pan until they begin to splutter, indicating they are toasted.
2. Allow the seeds to cool down, then transfer them to a blender. Blend briefly to create a coarse powder.
3. Add the powdered jaggery to the blender and blend again until the mixture becomes slightly sticky, utilising the natural oils from the sesame seeds.
4. Take small amounts of the mixture and roll them into balls.
5. Enjoy these energy-boosting seed balls as a snack.

Energise your day with these simple yet powerful sesame seed balls, a perfect blend of taste and traditional health benefits

Enhances bone health and immune function with essential minerals, boosts heart health and energy levels, and offers a healthy, natural snack alternative.

Sweet Coconut Jaggery Bites

Ingredients

Fresh Coconut (1 cup)
(USF, F, Manganese)
Green Cardamom (1 or 2)
(Mg, Zn, Ca, VitC)
Unrefined Jaggery (½ cup) *(Iron, Mg, Potassium)*

Notes

These coconut bars are a delightful way to enjoy the natural sweetness of coconut and jaggery, enhanced by the aromatic flavour of cardamom.

Instructions

1. Press and split open the cardamom pods, then add them to a hot pan.
2. Add shredded fresh coconut to the pan and dry roast it until the moisture evaporates and a pleasant aroma is released.
3. Incorporate the crushed jaggery into the mixture, stirring continuously.
4. Once combined, transfer the mixture to a blender and blend until it binds together.
5. Shape the mixture into small balls or spread it onto a tray to cut into desired sizes and shapes.
6. Allow the balls to cool before storing them in a glass jar.

Savour the exotic blend of coconut and cardamom in these delightful balls, a sweet and nutritious treat to uplift your spirits

Promotes heart health and digestion with healthy fats and fibre, boosts energy and metabolism, and offers a healthy snack alternative with anti-inflammatory benefits.

Delicious Foxtail Millet Pudding

Ingredients

Foxtail Millets (1/2 cup, washed
and soaked for 6-8 hours)
(PbP, F, Mg, B Vitamins)
**Unrefined Palm Jaggery or Date
Syrup** (to taste, ½ cup or less)
(Iron, Mg, Potassium)
**Coconut Milk or Any Plant-Based
Milk** (½ cup)
(USF, VitE, F)
Cardamom (2 pods)
(Mg, Zn, Ca, VitC)
Nuts for Garnishing
(PbP, Mg, USF, VitE)

Instructions

1. Cook the soaked foxtail millets in double the quantity of water on low heat until they become soft and the water is absorbed.
2. Once the millets are cooked, add the unrefined palm jaggery or date syrup, and mix well.
3. Add coconut milk or your preferred plant-based milk to the millets, stirring continuously.
4. Crush the cardamom pods and add them to the kheer for flavour.
5. Garnish with finely chopped nuts of your choice.
6. Serve warm or chilled, as preferred.

Indulge in the subtly sweet and comforting taste of foxtail millet kheer, a dessert that marries traditional flavours with the goodness of millets.

Boosts heart health and digestion with healthy fats and fibre, supports blood sugar management, and offers a nutritious, plant-based sweet treat with anti-inflammatory properties

Nature's Candy Bowl

Nature's Candy is a delightful way to enjoy the natural sweetness of fruits, keeping in mind the importance of not mixing different fruit groups for optimal digestion and absorption of nutrients.

Sweet Fruits

Eat separately or combine within this group

- Banana, Avocado, Dates
- Persimmon with Figs
- Papaya and Dates

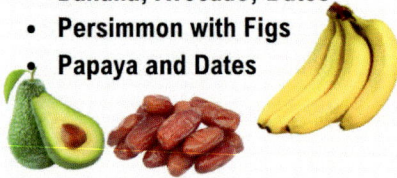

Acidic

Eat separately or combine within this group

- Oranges and Kiwi
- Pomegranate with Cranberries
- Pineapple and Grapefruit

Sub- Acidic

Eat separately or combine within this group

- Strawberries with Grapes
- Blueberries, Peach, and Pear
- Plum, Apricot, and Raspberry

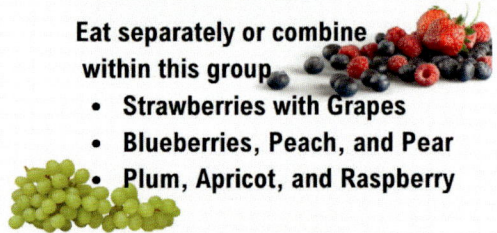

Melons (Eat separately): Watermelon, Cantaloupe, Honeydew (consume these on their own due to their high water content)

This approach to fruit consumption allows for better digestion and enjoyment of the natural flavours and nutrients each fruit offers.

Satvic Gaucamole

Ingredients

Avocados (2)
(USF, VitK, VitC, F)
Red Capsicum (1)
(VitC, AO, VitA)
Courgette (½)
(VitC, Potassium, Manganese)
Mint Leaves (½ Bunch)
(VitA, Iron, Folate)
Basil Leaves (½ Bunch)
(VitK, VitA, Mg)
Lemon Slice (1/2)
(VitC, VitB6, F)

Instructions

1. Blend the red capsicum, courgette, mint, and basil leaves into a fine puree.
2. Cut, stone, and scoop out the avocados. Mash them thoroughly.
3. Mix the avocado mash with the puree.
4. Squeeze in the juice from the lemon slice for added zest.
5. Garnish with small pieces of red capsicum and mint leaves, and serve in a bowl.

Perfect for those seeking a light yet satisfying vegan option that is both delicious and healthful

Boosts heart health and immunity with healthy fats and vitamins from avocados, and offers a light, refreshing vegan option rich in antioxidants and essential nutrients.

Fresh Sprout and Vegetable Medley

Ingredients

Any Sprouts like Mung Bean or Adzuki Bean Sprouts (1 cup)
(PbP, F, VitC)
Choice of Vegetables: Carrot, Beetroot, Cabbage, Coconut
(Various Vitamins and Minerals)
Seasoning: Pepper, Dry Mango Powder
Garnish: Coriander Leaves

Instructions

1. Take raw sprouts, add grated vegetables like carrot, beetroot, and cabbage and eat it straight away.
2. Alternatively steam the chosen sprouts until soft. Add grated vegetables like carrot, beetroot, and cabbage to the sprouts. Continue to steam for 5-10 minutes.
3. Season the mixture with pepper and dry mango powder.
4. Enhance the flavour with any spices or roasted seeds powder as desired.
5. Garnish the chat with grated coconut and fresh coriander leaves before serving.

This dish is a delightful way to enjoy sprouts, offering a blend of textures and flavours that's both satisfying and healthful.

Enhances digestive health with plant-based protein and fibre from sprouts, and offers a light, nutritious meal rich in vitamins and minerals for overall wellness.

Crunchy Veggie Sticks with Chickpea Hummus

Carrot (1) *(VitA, VitK, VitB6, F)*
Celery (2 Sticks) *(VitA, VitK, F, K)*
Parsnip (1) *(F, VitC, Folate, Potassium)*
Asparagus (2 Stalks)
(VitK, VitA, Folate, F)
Brown Chickpeas (½ cup)
(PbP, F, Mg, Iron)
Lemon Juice (2 Tablespoons)
(VitC, VitB6, F)
Sesame Seeds Paste (Roasted and
Pureed) *(Ca, Mg, PbP)*
Cold Pressed Extra Virgin Olive Oil or
Sesame Oil (1 Tablespoon)
(USF, VitE, Antioxidants)

Instructions

1. Soak, rinse, and cook the brown chickpeas.
2. Wash and cut the carrot, asparagus, parsnip, and celery into thin, finger-sized sticks and steam them.
3. Blend the cooked chickpeas with sesame seed paste.
4. Add olive oil or sesame oil, a pinch of salt (if needed), and lemon juice to the chickpea mixture and blend again.
5. Serve the hummus in a bowl accompanied by the steamed vegetable sticks for dipping.

Indulge in the fresh crunch of vegetables paired with the rich, creamy texture of homemade hummus.

Offers plant-based protein and healthy fats from chickpeas and sesame seeds, with a vitamin-rich vegetable mix for a nutritious, light snack that supports overall health.

Savoury Lentil Snack Fries

Ingredients

Lentils of Your Choice
(e.g., **Green Lentils, Marrow,
Lentilles Vertes, Mung Lentils**)
(PbP, F, Iron, Mg)

Instructions

1. Choose your preferred type of lentils (such as green lentils, marrow, lentilles vertes, or mung lentils or green grams).
2. Wash, soak overnight, rinse, and steam cook the lentils for 15-20 minutes until they are soft & firm but not mushy.
3. Remove from the heat and spread the lentils on a cloth to cool and dry.
4. Dry roast the half-cooked lentils and sprinkle with your favorite spice powder for added flavour.
5. Enjoy these crunchy lentil savouries as a snack or as a topping on salads and veggies.

Customise the spices according to your taste preference for a personalised snacking experience.

Provides a nutrient-dense snack with high plant-based protein, fibre, and essential minerals from lentils, offering a healthy alternative to processed snacks.

Healthy Millet Flakes Chivda

Ingredients

Finger Millet Flakes (1 cup)
(Ca, F, Fe, PbP)
Green Cabbage (¼ portion)
(VitK, VitC, F, AO)
Carrot (1)
(VitA, VitK, VitB6, F)
Fresh Garden Peas (½ cup)
(PbP, VitC, VitK, F)
Coriander Leaves (A Small Bunch)
(VitC, VitK, VitA, Iron)
Spices (**Mustard Seeds, Cumin
Seeds, Asafoetida, Turmeric Powder,
Curry Leaves, Urad Dal, Ginger,
Pepper or Green Chillies**)
Kelp (Salt Substitute)

Instructions

1. Lightly sprinkle water on the finger millet flakes to soften them.
2. In a heavy-bottomed pan, dry roast the spices one by one until aromatic.
3. Wash and grate the cabbage and carrot, and add them to the pan. Steam until soft.
4. Add the peas and cook until tender.
5. Garnish the chivda with chopped coriander leaves and sprinkle with kelp for seasoning.
6. Serve the chivda as a nutritious breakfast or light snack.

Reinvent your chivda with different varieties of millet flakes.

Enhances digestion and blood sugar control with fibre-rich finger millet flakes, supports thyroid health with iodine-rich kelp, and offers a nutritious, plant-based snack.

Homemade Airfried Corn Delight

Ingredients

Corn Kernels (½ cup)
(VitC, VitB1, F, C)

Instructions

1. Preheat a heavy-bottomed vessel with a see-through glass lid on high temperature.
2. Add corn kernels and then reduce the heat.
3. Regularly shake the vessel off the heat to prevent burning, until all kernels have popped.
4. Enjoy the popcorn immediately after it's prepared.

Experience the simple pleasure of popping your own healthy, airfried popcorn – a timeless snack for all occasions.

Opt for organic corn kernels to avoid genetically modified crops. This easy recipe offers a healthier alternative to traditional popcorn without compromising on taste

Easy Hemp Seed Energy Balls

Ingredients

Hemp Seed Hearts (1 cup)
(PbP, OMG3, Mg)

Dates (4-5)
(F, VitB6, Potassium)

Instructions

1. Combine hemp seed hearts and dates in a blender.
2. Pulse until the mixture is coarse and sticky, suitable for forming balls.
3. Roll the mixture with your hands to form small balls.
4. Enjoy these nutrient-packed bites anytime for a quick energy boost.

Quick, nutritious, and delicious – these hemp seed balls are your go-to snack for a healthy lift

Incorporate roasted flaxseeds or sesame seeds powder for added nutrients, or use palm or unrefined jaggery as an alternative to dates.

Homemade Fresh Fruit Ice Pops

Ingredients

**Any Water-Rich Fruits
(e.g., Oranges, Melon)**

Instructions

1. Extract juice from the oranges or your chosen fruits.
2. Dilute the juice with water to suit your taste preferences.
3. Pour the mixture into fruit lolly holders.
4. Freeze for about 4 hours or until solid.
5. Enjoy these homemade fruit lollies as a perfect cool-down treat.

Ideal as a refreshing, low-calorie treat, these lollies are perfect for hot days and provide a delightful way to increase your fruit intake.

These natural fruit lollies offer a healthier alternative to commercial ice pops, free from artificial colours and sweeteners.

Savoury Moth Bean Veggie Patties

Ingredients

Moth Beans (½ cup, washed and soaked overnight)
(PbP, F, Iron, Potassium)

Mixed Vegetables (Carrots, Capsicum, Peas, Cauliflower)
(Various Vitamins and Minerals)

Green Leafy Vegetables (Coriander or Parsley Leaves, Mint Leaves)
(VitC, VitK, Iron, AO)

Essential Spices: Turmeric, Cumin Seeds, Pepper, Ginger, Dry Mango Powder

Roasted Flaxseed Powder (1 spoon)
(Omega-3 Fatty Acids, F, PbP

Instructions

1. Steam cook the moth beans in double the quantity of water until they are soft.
2. Blend the cooked beans to a dough-like consistency, using minimal or no water.
3. Mix chopped mixed vegetables, green leafy vegetables, flaxseed powder, and spices into the moth bean dough.
4. Shape the mixture into lemon-sized balls and flatten them into circular patties.
5. Roast the cutlets on both sides on a tava or pan until they are golden and crispy.
6. Serve the cutlets with mint chutney.

Indulge in the goodness of moth beans and veggies, crafted into delightful cutlets for your enjoyment.

Boosts energy and heart health with plant-based protein, fibre, and omega-3 fatty acids, and enhances immune support with a variety of vitamins and in a healthy, plant-based cutlet.

Steamed Soup & Veggies

Soothing Butternut and Sugar Snap Soup

Ingredients:

Butternut Squash (½)
(VitA, VitC, Potassium, F)
Sugar Snaps (10) *(PbP, VitC, Iron, F)*
Brazil Nut or Almond Milk (⅓ cup) *(USF, VitE, Mg)*
Seasoning: **Pepper, Dulse** (Seaweed, rich in Iodine and Minerals)
Herbs: **Oregano, Thyme** (Antioxidants, flavour)

Instructions:

1. Wash and steam the butternut squash pieces and sugar snaps until they are soft.
2. Once soft, mash the vegetables and add Brazil nut or almond milk to achieve a creamy texture.
3. Season the soup with pepper and dulse for a savoury touch.
4. Garnish with oregano and thyme for added flavour.
5. Optionally, you can swap butternut squash with pumpkin for a different variation of this creamy soup.

Note:

This soup is a delightful and nutritious meal, perfect for a cozy evening.

Supports vision and immune health with vitamins A and C, aids in cardiovascular health and digestion, and offers a nutritious, plant-based soup with thyroid-boosting iodine.

Holy Horse Gram Lentil Soup with Artichoke

Ingredients:

Horse Gram Lentils (½ cup, washed and soaked overnight)
(PbP, F, Iron, Calcium)
Artichoke (1, washed, with edges snipped)
(VitC, VitK, F, Mg)
Basil Leaves (1 Bunch)
(VitA, VitK, AO, Mg)
Seasoning: **Pepper, Kelp or Raw Mango Powder**
(Iodine, Vitamins, Minerals)

Instructions:

1. Steam cook the soaked horse gram lentils until they are soft.
2. In a separate pot or steamer, steam the artichoke pieces until tender.
3. Mash the cooked lentils and add the steamed artichoke.
4. Season the soup with pepper and kelp or raw mango powder to taste.
5. Garnish with fresh basil leaves and optional soaked seeds or nuts before serving.

Note:

This soup combines the earthy taste of horse gram lentils with the subtle flavours of artichoke, making it a wholesome and satisfying meal.

Boosts heart health and aids weight loss with high protein and fibre, and offers a comforting, plant-based meal rich in vitamins and antioxidants.

Hearty Green Cabbage and Peas Broth

Ingredients:

Green Cabbage (½ portion)
(VitK, VitC, F, AO)
Peas (1 cup)
(PbP, VitC, F, VitK)
Parsnip (1)
(F, VitC, Folate, Potassium)
Ginger (1 inch piece)
(Mg, Zn, K)
Peppercorns (1 teaspoon)
(K, VitA, VitC, AO)
Cumin Seeds (1 teaspoon)
(Iron, Mg, Ca)
Coriander Leaves (A Small Bunch)
(VitC, VitK, VitA, Iron)

Instructions:

1. Wash and steam the cabbage, parsnip, and peas until they are soft.
2. Either mash the steamed vegetables or blend them along with coriander leaves to create a smooth texture.
3. Season the soup with crushed peppercorns and cumin seeds for added flavour.
4. Serve this light yet hearty soup warm, ideal for a healthy meal or appetiser.

Enhances immune health, supports digestion and heart health with high fibre and protein, and offers a light yet comforting, nutrient-rich meal.

Nourishing Moringa and Mung Dal Broth

Ingredients:

Moringa Leaves (1 Bunch)
(VitA, VitC, Calcium, Iron)
Grated Coconut (1/4 Cup)
(USF, F, Manganese)
Mung Dal (Split Yellow Lentils) (½ Cup, Soaked)
(PbP, F, Mg, K)
Tempering Spices: Asafoetida, Mustard Seeds, Urad Dal, Cumin Seeds, Curry Leaves, Peppercorns, Ginger, Green Chillies, Turmeric Powder, Dulse or Sea Salt *(Various Nutrients and Antioxidants)*

Instructions:

1. Prepare the mung dal by washing and cooking it until soft.
2. In a medium-hot pan, add the tempering ingredients – asafoetida, mustard seeds, urad dal, cumin seeds, curry leaves, peppercorns, ginger, green chillies, and turmeric powder.
3. Once the tempering is aromatic, add the moringa leaves to the pan. Allow them to steam and cook with the spices.
4. Season the mixture with pepper and dulse or sea salt to taste.
5. Near the end of cooking, stir in the grated coconut.
6. Combine the cooked mung dal with the moringa mixture and serve hot.

Enhances overall health with a nutrient-rich blend of moringa and mung dal, offering antioxidants, protein, and digestive benefits in a creamy, energy-boosting soup.

Velvety Sweet Potato Soup with Leek and Chives

Ingredients:

Leek (1)
(VitK, VitA, VitC, F)
Sweet Potato (1)
(VitA, VitC, Potassium, F)
Ginger (1 inch piece)
(Mg, Zn, K)
Coconut Milk (1/4 cup)
(USF, VitC, Iron)
Chives (A few strands)
(VitK, VitC, Folate)

Instructions:

1. Wash, peel, and cut the sweet potato. Wash and chop the leek and ginger.
2. Steam the sweet potato, leek, and ginger until they are soft.
3. Once cooked, mash the mixture until smooth.
4. Stir in the chopped chives and add your choice of seasonings.
5. For a creamier texture, add coconut milk or your preferred plant-based nut milk.
6. Serve this soup warm, garnished with additional chives if desired.

Boosts bone, eye, and immune health with vitamins A, C, K; supports heart and digestive wellness in a creamy, plant-based, soothing soup

Broccoli Carrot Soup with Perpetual Spinach

Ingredients:

Broccoli (with stems and leaves) (½)
(VitC, VitK, F, AO)
Carrot (1 or 2)
(VitA, VitK, VitB6, F)
Perpetual Spinach (A Bunch)
(VitA, VitC, Iron, Ca)
Seasoning: **Pepper, Salt** (as required)

Instructions:

1. Wash and cut the broccoli, including stems and leaves, and the carrots.
2. Steam the broccoli and carrots until they are soft.
3. Once cooked, add the perpetual spinach leaves and let them wilt with the residual heat. Turn off the heat.
4. Mash the vegetable mixture to a desired consistency.
5. Season the soup with pepper and salt to taste.
6. Serve this warm and nourishing soup as a healthy meal option.

Enhances immune and cardiovascular health, promotes eye and skin vitality, and offers a light, nutrient-dense, plant-based meal with sustainable options

Hearty Sweet Potato and Kale Platter

Ingredients:

Sweet Potato (1)
(F, AO, VitA, VitC)
Fresh Green Peas or Overnight Soaked and Cooked Dry Peas
(PbP, VitK, VitC)
Kale Leaves (50-100 gms)
(VitK, VitA, VitC, AO)
Organic Tofu
(PbP, Iron, Ca)
Nutritional Yeast
(B12, PbP, GF)
Lemon Juice
(VitC, DH)

> Enhances digestive health, immune function, and bone density with a mix of sweet potato, kale, tofu, and seeds in a nutrient-rich, plant-based meal.

Instructions:

1. Wash, cut, and steam the sweet potato with 1 tbsp water in a pan.
2. After about 10 minutes, add the washed kale leaves.
3. Blend tofu, nutritional yeast, and lemon juice in a blender to create a sauce-like consistency.
4. Ensure the sweet potato and kale are cooked to desired softness while retaining their colour.
5. Peel the sweet potato and arrange it on a plate with the kale leaves and peas.
6. Drizzle the tofu sauce over the vegetables and serve.

Note:

Those with thyroid conditions should moderate their kale intake to avoid potential interference with iodine absorption.

Hearty Butternut and Sprouts Delight

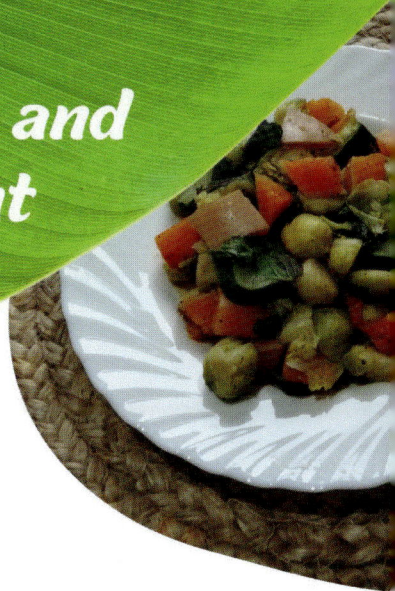

Ingredients:

Butternut Squash (¼ size)
(VitA, VitC, F, Potassium)
Brussels Sprouts (2 handfuls)
(VitK, VitC, F, AO)
Asparagus
(VitK, VitA, F, Folate)
Roasted Seeds or Nuts Powder (e.g., Sesame, Flax Seeds, Pistachios)
(PbP, Mg, USF, VitE)

Instructions:

1. Wash and cut the butternut squash, Brussels sprouts, and asparagus to the desired size.
2. Place the vegetables in a pan with ¼ cup of water, cover with a lid, and steam until soft.
3. Once cooked, sprinkle with a choice of roasted sesame seeds, flax seeds, or pistachio nuts powder.
4. Serve as is or accompany with a side like parsnip mint chutney for added flavour.

Note:

Butternut squash can be cooked with its skin on for additional nutrients.

Boosts vision, immunity, and digestion with a mix of squash, Brussels sprouts, and asparagus, offering heart and bone benefits in a nutrient-rich meal.

Beetroot and Courgette Harmony

Ingredients:

Beetroot (1)
(F, VitC, Iron, Mg)
Courgette (Zucchini) (1)
(VitA, VitC, Potassium, F)
Beetroot Leaves (Taken from Beetroot)
(VitK, VitA, VitC, Mg)
Coconut Kernels (2)
(USF, F, Manganese)
Fennel Seeds (1 teaspoon)
(VitC, Ca, Iron, Mg)
Ginger Piece (1 inch, sliced)
(Mg, Zn, K)

Enhances cardiovascular and digestive health with beetroot, courgette, and fennel seeds, offering detoxifying and antioxidant benefits in a balanced meal.

Instructions:

1. Wash and steam the beetroot until slightly softened.
2. Add courgette, coconut pieces, and beetroot leaves, as they cook quickly.
3. After 2-3 minutes, remove some beetroot pieces, coconut kernels, and beet leaves, allowing them to cool.
4. Blend the beet leaves, coconut, cooked beetroot pieces, fennel seeds, and ginger to create the chutney.
5. Serve the steamed vegetables with the freshly made beet leaves chutney.

Note:

Coconut can be substituted with a base of parsnip, nuts, or seeds for different flavours and textures.

Garden Fresh Veggies with Celery Dip

Ingredients:

Carrot (1) *(VitA, VitK, VitB6, F)*
French Beans (6-7) *(VitA, VitC, F, Iron)*
Fresh Green Peas (2 tablespoons) *(PbP, VitC, VitK, F)*
Celery Stalks with Leaves (2) *(VitA, VitK, F, K)*
Ginger (1 1.5 inch size) *(Mg, Zn, K)*
Red Capsicum (1 small) *(VitC, VitA, AO)*
Gooseberry or ½ a Lemon *(VitC, VitB6, F)*
Cumin Seeds *(Digestion, Iron)*
Black Peppercorns *(K, VitA, VitC, AO)*
Coriander Leaves (Generous Bunch) *(VitC, VitK, VitA, F)*

Instructions:

1. Wash and prepare all the vegetables.
2. Cut the celery, ginger, and capsicum into small pieces. Steam them with a few peppercorns and 2-3 tablespoons of water until soft.
3. Once cooled, blend the steamed celery mixture with lemon slices or gooseberry to create a chutney.
4. Snip the tails of carrots and beans, cutting them into thin, long vertical strips. Add fresh green peas, pepper, cumin seeds, and coriander leaves.
5. Once soft, arrange the steamed vegetables on a plate and serve with the celery chutney.

Supports vision and immune health with vitamin-rich vegetables, aids digestion and cardiovascular wellness, and offers a balanced, antioxidant-rich meal for overall well-being.

Moringa Infused Vegetable Stir Fry

Ingredients:

Asparagus (8-10 stalks)
(VitK, VitA, Folate, K)
Cauliflower (¼ of a full portion)
(VitC, VitK, F, AO)
Moringa Leaves (A Big Bunch)
(VitA, VitC, Ca, Iron)
Urad Dal/Lentils (2 tablespoons)
(PbP, F, Mg, Iron)
Green Chillies (2)
(VitC, Capsaicin, AO)
Optional: Coconut (Shredded) *(USF, F, Manganese),*Cumin Seeds *(Digestion, Iron)*, Mustard Seeds *(Mg, Ca, K, AO)*, Asafoetida Powder (1 pinch) *(Digestion)*, Turmeric Powder (1 teaspoon) *(Curcumin, AO)*

Instructions:

> Enhances bone health, vision, and immune function, offers anti-inflammatory and digestive benefits, and provides a nutritious, plant-based meal for overall wellness.

1. Wash all vegetables thoroughly.
2. Remove the leaves from the moringa (drumstick) stalks.
3. Cut the cauliflower and asparagus into desired sizes and steam them with turmeric powder and cumin seeds.
4. In a separate pan, heat mustard seeds and cumin seeds until they splutter. Add urid dal and asafoetida, cooking until aromatic. Then, add slit green chillies and moringa leaves.
5. Add a few tablespoons of water to the pan to prevent sticking, and steam the mixture until soft.
6. Add shredded coconut, cover with a lid, and turn off the heat.
7. Season with a little salt to taste.

Colourful Cabbage and Capsicum

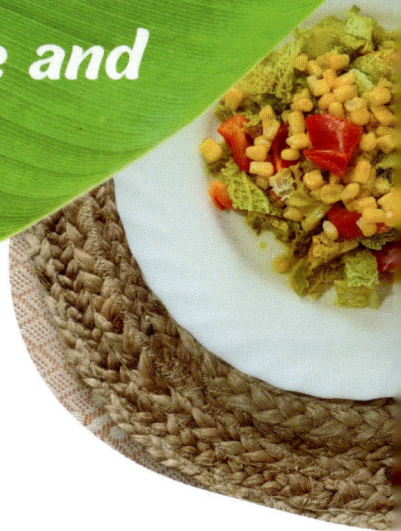

Ingredients:

Cabbage (¼ portion)
(VitC, VitK, AO, F)
Spinach (Bunch of Leaves)
(VitA, VitC, Iron, Ca)
Orange Capsicum (1)
(VitC, VitA, AO)
Sweetcorn (A Handful) or Edamame Beans
(PbP, VitC, VitK, F)

Instructions:

1. Wash and steam the cabbage until it begins to soften.
2. Add slices of orange capsicum and sweetcorn or edamame beans to the steamer after the cabbage has slightly softened.
3. When the vegetables are almost cooked, add the spinach leaves and immediately switch off the flame. The residual steam will cook the spinach.
4. Season with salt and pepper to taste.
5. Optionally, serve with a white sauce or dressing for enhanced flavour.

Boosts cardiovascular health and immune function, supports bone density and blood health, and promotes digestion and overall well-being with a nutrient-rich, plant-based meal.

Brain Boosting Broccoli and Brahmi Feast

Ingredients:

Broccoli (½ with stem)
(VitC, VitK, F, AO)
Carrot (1)
(VitA, VitK, VitB6, F)
Brahmi Leaves (A Bunch)
(Antioxidants, Bacosides)
Grated Coconut (A Fistful)
(USF, F, Manganese)
Cumin Seeds (1 teaspoon)
(Iron, Mg, Ca)
Fennel Seeds (1 teaspoon)
(VitC, Ca, Iron, Mg)
Peppercorns
(K, VitA, VitC, AO)
Gooseberry or ½ Lemon Slice (VitC, VitB6, F)
Soaked Sunflower Seeds (2 tablespoons)
(PbP, VitE, Mg, USF)

> Boosts cognitive and digestive health, supports vision and heart health, and combats oxidative stress with a nutrient-rich, flavour-enhanced meal.

Instructions:

1. Wash and steam the Brahmi leaves with cumin, fennel seeds, and peppercorns until they soften while retaining their green colour.
2. Add grated coconut or sunflower seeds in the final 2 minutes of steaming.
3. Once cooled, blend this mixture with deseeded gooseberry or lemon slices to create the chutney.
4. Simultaneously, steam the cut broccoli and carrot.
5. Arrange the steamed vegetables on a plate, top with the Brahmi leaves chutney, and sprinkle with sunflower seeds.

Olives Infused Cauliflower Delight

Ingredients:

Cauliflower (Around 10 Medium-Size Florets)
(VitC, VitK, F, AO)
Cumin Seeds (1 teaspoon)
(Iron, Mg, Ca)
Turmeric Powder (½ teaspoon)
(Curcumin, AO)
Red Cabbage (¼ Portion, Cut into Small Pieces)
(VitC, VitK, AO, F)
Celery (2 Stalks) *(VitA, VitK, F, K)*
Green Olives (5-6) *(VitE, Iron, Copper, fibre)*

Instructions:

1. Wash the cauliflower, celery, and red cabbage.
2. Cut the red cabbage into small pieces, celery stalks into 2-inch pieces, and retain the small floret shapes of the cauliflower.
3. Place the vegetables in a thick-bottomed karahi or kadai. Sprinkle with cumin seeds and turmeric powder, add a bit of water, cover with a lid, and cook on a low flame.
4. Once cooked and soft, arrange the cabbage leaves on a plate to form a bed, and then decorate with cauliflower florets, celery sticks, and washed olives.
5. Season with pepper, unrefined sea salt or Himalayan salt, and any herbal leaves like basil as desired.

Enhances digestive and immune health, supports heart health with antioxidants and healthy fats, and offers anti-inflammatory benefits in a nutritious, plant-based meal.

Soothing Bottle Gourd & Spinach Mix

Ingredients:

Bottle Gourd (1 small size)
(VitC, VitK, Ca, Potassium)
Spinach Leaves (50 100 gms)
(VitA, VitC, Iron, Ca)
Chestnuts (5-6)
(VitC, VitB6, F, Mg)
Turmeric Powder (1 pinch)
(Curcumin, AO)
Black Pepper Powder (1 teaspoon) or Green Chillies (2, slit at the centre)
(Capsaicin, VitC, AO)
Black Cumin Seeds (1 teaspoon)
(Iron, Ca, AO)

Instructions:

1. Wash and cut the bottle gourd into medium-sized pieces.
2. In the pan, cook the bottle gourd with turmeric powder and either black pepper or green chillies.
3. Once the gourd is cooked, add spinach leaves and chestnuts. Then, switch off the heat. The residual steam will cook the spinach.
4. Serve on a plate as a standalone vegetable meal or pair it with lentils like mung dal for added protein and texture.

Supports gut health and boosts immunity with high vitamins C and K, provides hydration and anti-inflammatory benefits in a low-calorie, nutrient-rich meal

Celeriac and Courgette Veggie Medley

Ingredients:

Celeriac (½ portion)
(VitK, VitC, Phosphorus, F)
Courgette (Zucchini) (1)
(VitA, VitC, Potassium, F)
Mangetout/Snow Pea/Sugar Snap Pea (5-6)
(VitC, VitK, Fibre, Protein)
Fennel Bulb (1)
(VitC, Fibre, Potassium, F)
Parsley Leaves (½ Fresh Bunch)
(VitC, VitK, VitA, Iron)
Seasoning: Turmeric, Pepper, Salt, Oregano
Soaked Pumpkin Seeds and Hazelnuts
(PbP, Mg, VitE, USF)

Instructions:

1. Wash all vegetables thoroughly.
2. Peel and cut the celeriac into small cubes.
3. Wash and cut courgette, mangetout, and fennel bulb.
4. Steam all the cut vegetables together, including the celeriac.
5. Toward the end of steaming, add the seasonings, parsley leaves, and soaked seeds and nuts. Steam for a couple more minutes.
6. Arrange the steamed vegetables on a plate. Serve as is or with a side of mint sauce.

Boosts bone health and immunity with vitamins K and C, aids digestion and heart health with high fibre, and offers a nutrient-rich, plant-based meal with antioxidant benefits.

Cooked Whole Grain Meals

Quinoa with Broccoli & Squash Seeds Chutney

Ingredients

Quinoa (1 cup, washed and soaked for 6-8 hours)
(PbP, Mg, F, VitB)

Broccoli (½, with stems and leaves)
(VitC, VitK, F, AO)

Butternut Squash (Save the seeds for chutney)
(VitA, VitC, Potassium, F)

Coconut Kernels (2 or 3) or alternative seeds/nuts
(USF, F, Manganese)

Cumin Seeds or Black Cumin Seeds (1 teaspoon)
(Iron, Mg, Ca)

Instructions

1. Cook the soaked quinoa in 2 cups of water on low heat for about 20 minutes until all the water is absorbed.

2. Wash and cut the butternut squash and broccoli stems. In a separate vessel, steam these along with the butternut squash seeds, coconut (or alternative seeds/nuts), and cumin seeds.

3. Once soft, remove the vessel with the seeds, coconut, and broccoli stems, and let them cool.

4. Blend these ingredients to make a chutney.

5. Serve the cooked quinoa on a plate along with the steamed vegetables, and accompany it with the broccoli and squash seeds chutney.

Notes
Coconut can be substituted with sunflower seeds, peanuts, or sesame seeds for different flavours and textures.

Provides complete protein and fibre, supports cardiovascular and immune health, and offers a nutrient-rich, plant-based option for overall well-being with quinoa, vegetables, and seeds

Nutritious Little Millet Pongal Feast

Ingredients

Little Millets (1 cup, washed and soaked for 6-8 hours)
(PbP, F, Mg, B Vitamins)

Split Moong Dal with Skin (½ cup, washed and soaked)
(PbP, F, Mg, K)

Cumin Seeds
(Digestion, Iron)

Peppercorns
(K, VitA, VitC, AO)

Seasoning: Mustard Seeds, Curry Leaves, Ginger, Asafoetida
(Digestion, AO)

Cold Pressed Sesame Seed Oil or Groundnut or Coconut Oil

Instructions

1. Cook the soaked millets and moong dal in 4 cups of water on low heat until they form a pongal-like consistency.

2. In a separate pan, heat the oil and add asafoetida, mustard seeds, cumin seeds, peppercorns, pepper powder, curry leaves, and ginger.

3. Once the mustard seeds splutter and the spices are slightly roasted, add this mixture to the cooked millet pongal.

4. Serve the pongal with coconut chutney and steamed vegetables.

Notes

This dish offers a delightful combination of textures and flavours, making it a satisfying and nutritious meal option.

Boosts digestion and heart health with high-fibre millets and moong dal, maintains balanced blood sugar, and offers antioxidant-rich, plant-based well-being with flavourful spices.

Exotic Black Rice and Vegetable Curry

Ingredients

Black Rice
(1 cup, washed and soaked for 6-8 hours)
(Antioxidants, PbP, F)

Bottle Gourd (½ portion)
(VitC, VitK, Ca, Potassium)

Red Capsicum (1)
(VitC, VitA, AO)

Parsley Leaves (1 Bunch)
(VitC, VitK, VitA, Iron)

Cumin Seeds
(Digestion, Iron)

Peppercorns
(K, VitA, VitC, AO)
Optional Seasoning:
Mustard Seeds, Curry Leaves, Turmeric Powder, Ginger, Asafoetida

Optional: 1 spoon of cold-pressed Sesame Seed, Groundnut, or Coconut Oil

Instructions

1. Cook the soaked black rice in 2 cups of water on low heat until all the water is absorbed and the rice is cooked.

2. Wash, cut, and steam the bottle gourd and capsicum with turmeric powder, peppercorns, and cumin seeds.

3. In another vessel, dry roast asafoetida, mustard seeds, cumin seeds, peppercorns, curry leaves, and ginger.

4. Once the mustard seeds splutter and the spices are slightly roasted, add the steamed bottle gourd and capsicum.

5. Serve this vegetable curry alongside the cooked black rice with a side of parsley chutney.

Notes

Cold-pressed oil can be added at the end for additional flavour and nutritional benefits, especially for children.

Supports heart, kidney, and blood health, boosts immunity and skin health, and offers a hydrating, antioxidant-rich, plant-based meal with black rice and vegetables.

Exotic Mung Bean Dosa with Ridge Gourd Chutney

Ingredients

Ridge Gourd (1, scraped at the edges)
(VitC, VitA, Iron, Zinc)
Green Chillies (2)
(VitC, Capsaicin, AO)
Celery Stalk (1)
(VitA, VitK, F, K)
Ginger (1 inch)
(Mg, Zn, K)
Coriander Leaves
(A Small Bunch)
(VitC, VitK, VitA, Iron)
Curry Leaves (4-5)
(Carb, Protein, F)
Soaked and Peeled Almonds (4-5)
(PbP, VitE, Mg, USF)
Fennel Seeds (Saunf) (1 pinch)
(VitC, Ca, Iron, Mg)
Cumin Seeds (1 pinch)
(Iron, Mg, Ca)
Turmeric Powder (1 pinch) *(Curcumin, AO)*

For Dosa Batter 1 cup
Mung Beans

Instructions

Instructions for Chutney:
1. Wash and scrape the rough ridges of the ridge gourd, cutting it into small pieces. Reserve the scraped peelings for another use.

2. Steam the ridge gourd pieces with slit green chillies, ginger, celery stalk, cumin seeds, fennel seeds, and turmeric powder.

3. Once cooked, add the almonds and coriander leaves. Let it cool.

4. Blend the mixture into a smooth chutney.

5. Do a seasoning of dry roasted mustard seeds and curry leaves to add to the chutney.

Instructions for Dosa batter:
- Wash, rinse and soak 1 cup of mung beans overnight.
- Rinse and blend it with fennel seeds, cumin seeds, ½ inch ginger piece, ¼ tsp peppercorns or green chillies.
- Add water and make it into thick pourable consistency on the pan.
- Scoop a ladle full and add on a heated pan and spread into circles like a pancake.
- Once cooked and edges tend to leave the pan, flip on the other side.

Wholemeal Buckwheat Pancake

Ingredients

Buckwheat Flour (1 cup)
(F, PbP, VitB, Magnesium)

Flaxseed Powder (1 spoon)
(Omega-3 Fatty Acids, F, PbP)

Coriander Leaves or Other Green Leaves (1 bunch)
(VitC, VitK, Iron, F)

Cumin Seeds (1 pinch)
(Iron, Magnesium, Calcium)

Instructions

1. Wash and finely chop or grind the coriander leaves with some water.

2. Add the coriander mixture to the buckwheat flour. Incorporate flaxseed powder for added health benefits.

3. Gradually add about 2 cups of water to the flour mixture, adjusting to achieve a pourable consistency (neither too thick nor too runny).

4. Heat a tava or pan. Pour a ladleful of the batter onto the pan, using the back of the ladle to spread it in circular motions, forming a thin pancake.

5. Cook until the edges start to lift from the pan, then flip carefully with a spatula.

6. Serve the dosa or pancake with steamed vegetables and ridge gourd chutney.

Supports digestive health and energy levels with gluten-free buckwheat flour, promotes heart health with omega-3 rich flaxseeds, and offers a nutritious, plant-based meal rich in vitamins and minerals.

Wholesome Brown Rice Vegetable Pulav

Ingredients

Brown Rice (1 cup, washed and soaked for 8 hours)
(F, VitB, Magnesium, Selenium)
Mixed Vegetables (Carrots, Peas, Beans, Broccoli, Sweet Potato)
(Various Vitamins and Minerals)
Green Chillies (2-3)
(VitC, Capsaicin, AO)
Ginger (1 inch piece, crushed)
(Mg, Zn, K)
Dry Masala (Bay Leaves, Green and Black Cardamoms, Cinnamon Sticks, Star Anise, Cloves, Cumin Seeds)
(Various Nutrients and Antioxidants)
Curry Leaves (5-6)
(Carb, Protein, F)
Salt and Pepper (as per taste)
Coriander Leaves (1 bunch)
(VitC, VitK, VitA, Iron)
Mint Leaves (1 bunch)
(VitA, Folate, Iron)

Instructions

1. Cook the soaked brown rice in 2 cups of water on low heat until it's almost done.

2. In another pan, dry roast the masala items. Add the crushed ginger, curry leaves, and green chillies.

3. Add a little water to prevent sticking.

4. Once aromatic, add the washed and sliced mixed vegetables. Steam with some water, covered, to prevent sticking.

5. When the vegetables are slightly soft, add the almost cooked rice, salt, and pepper. Mix well.

6. Just before turning off the flame, stir in the chopped coriander and mint leaves.

7. Serve this pulav with plantain, swede, or any fried vegetable for added texture and flavour.

Nutrient Packed Red Rice Upma Delight

Ingredients

Flattened Red Rice (1 cup)
(F, VitB, Antioxidants, Iron)

**Vegetables of Choice
(Cauliflower, Peas,
Capsicum, Broad Beans,
etc.)**

Seasoning Ingredients:
Mustard Seeds, Curry
Leaves, Cumin Seeds, Urad
Dal, Peanuts, Ginger, Green
Chillies
Turmeric Powder
Salt and Pepper (to taste)
Coriander Leaves (for
garnish)
Mint Chutney

Instructions

1. Wash and soak flattened red rice in water for 5-10 minutes.

2. Dry roast the seasoning ingredients (mustard seeds, curry leaves, cumin seeds, urad dal, peanuts, ginger, and green chillies) in a pan.

3. Add your chosen chopped vegetables to the pan and cook until tender.

4. Once the vegetables are cooked, drain the soaked poha and add it to the pan.

5. Season with turmeric powder, salt, and pepper. Stir to mix well.

6. Garnish with fresh coriander leaves.

7. Serve the poha with a side of mint chutney.

Enhances digestion and blood sugar control with fibre-rich red rice poha, offers a nutritious mix of vitamins and minerals from vegetables, and combats oxidative stress for overall health.

Protein Packed Chickpea and Vegetable Medley

Ingredients

Brown Chickpeas (1/2 cup, washed and soaked overnight) *(PbP, F, Mg, Iron)*

Carrot (1) *(VitA, VitK, VitB6, F)*

Cabbage (½ portion) *(VitC, VitK, F, AO)*

Spices:
Cumin Seeds (½ teaspoon),
Turmeric Powder (1 pinch),
Asafoetida (1 tiny pinch),
Pepper Powder (as required),
Amchur or Dry Mango Powder (1 pinch)

Instructions

1. Cook the soaked brown chickpeas in 1 cup of water until soft.

2. Wash and cut the carrots and cabbage (or any other vegetable like in the picture above Butternut squash is used). Steam them separately.

3. Dry roast the spices (cumin seeds, turmeric powder, asafoetida, pepper powder, amchur) in a small pan and add them to the steamed vegetables.

4. Serve the dish with coconut mint chutney or homemade hummus. To make hummus, blend some of the cooked chickpeas with tahini, lemon juice, and optionally, garlic, to achieve a sauce-like consistency.

Boosts heart health and digestive wellness with protein-rich brown chickpeas, offers a blend of essential nutrients and antioxidants from carrots and cabbage, and provides plant-based protein.

Savoury Oatmeal with Fresh Greens

Ingredients

Whole Oat Groats (½ cup, soaked overnight)
(F, PbP, Mg, B Vitamins)

Celery Stalks (2 stalks)
(VitA, VitK, F, K)

Asparagus (5-6 sticks)
(VitK, VitA, Folate, K)

Spinach (A Bunch)
(VitA, VitC, Iron, Ca)

Optional Spices:
Pepper Powder (1 pinch),
Dry Mango Powder (for a salty taste)

Instructions

1. Cook the soaked whole oat groats in a pot on low heat until soft.

2. Meanwhile, wash and cut the celery stalks and asparagus into roughly three parts each.

3. Steam these vegetables with a pinch of pepper and dry mango powder for added flavour, if desired.

4. Once the vegetables are soft, add them on top of the cooked oats along with spinach for the last 2 minutes of cooking.

5. For an extra creamy texture, stir in your choice of plant-based milk before serving.

Supports heart health and digestive wellness with low-glycemic whole oats, offers a nutrient-rich start with iron and vitamin-packed spinach, and maintains overall health with vitamin-rich celery and asparagus.

Hearty Lentils with Dwarf Copper Leaves

Ingredients

Split Mung Dal/Lentils with Skin (½ cup, washed and soaked for 4-6 hours)
(PbP, F, Mg, K)

Dwarf Copper Leaves
(1 bunch, including stems)
(Vitamins, Minerals, Antioxidants)

Bottle Gourd or any Gourd Family Vegetables
(VitC, VitK, Ca, Potassium)

Spices:
Asafoetida (1 tiny pinch),
Mustard Seeds (½ teaspoon),
Cumin Seeds (½ teaspoon),
Turmeric Powder (1 pinch),
Curry Leaves (4-5)
Optional: Pepper and Dry Mango Powder for seasoning
Lemon Juice (for taste and nutrition)

Instructions

1. Steam and cook the mung dal until soft.

2. In another vessel, steam the washed and cut bottle gourd. Add dwarf copper leaves when the bottle gourd is nearly cooked.

3. In a medium-hot pan, roast spices one by one until aromatic. Start with mustard seeds, followed by cumin seeds, asafoetida, and curry leaves.

4. Add the cooked lentils and steamed leaves to the pan. Season with pepper and dry mango powder, if desired.

5. Before serving, squeeze fresh lemon juice over the dish to enhance the taste and nutrition.

Enhances heart health and digestion with protein-rich moong dal, supports eye health with nutritious dwarf copper leaves, and offers a hydrating, low-calorie meal with bottle gourd, enriched with anti-inflammatory spices and vitamin C for better iron absorption.

Vibrant Green Peas and Vegetable Kurma

Ingredients

Green Peas (½ cup, washed and soaked overnigt) *(PbP, VitC, F, K)*

Carrot (1) *(VitA, VitK, VitB6, F)*

Cauliflower (⅓ portion) *(VitC, VitK, F, AO)*

Broad Beans (1 handful) *(PbP, VitK, VitB6, Iron)*

Coconut Kernels (2 or 3) *(USF, F, Manganese)*

Poppy Seeds (1 tablespoon) *(Ca, Mg, PbP)*

Fennel Seeds (1 teaspoon) *(VitC, Ca, Iron, Mg)*

Tempering Spices: Bay Leaf, Cinnamon Stick, Cloves, Green Cardamom, Star Anise, Turmeric Powder, Cumin Seeds

Instructions

1. Cook the soaked green peas in a pot until tender.

2. In another pan, dry roast the tempering spices. Add washed and cut carrot, cauliflower florets, and broad beans. Cook on low heat until the vegetables are tender.

3. In a blender, create a puree of poppy seeds, coconut kernels, and fennel seeds with 3-4 tablespoons of water.

4. Once the peas are cooked, add them to the pan with the vegetables.

5. Stir in any homemade garam masala powder and coriander powder for additional flavour and thickness.

6. Add the coconut-poppy-fennel puree to the pan, cooking for an additional 2 minutes. Be careful not to boil the mixture too much.

7. Serve this kurma with rice or roti.

Savoury Cannellini Beans with Broad Beans and Kale

Ingredients

Cannellini Beans
(PbP, F, Mg, Iron)
Kale (100 gms)
(VitA, VitC, VitK, Ca)
Any Gourd Family Veg (1)
(VitA, VitC, Potassium, F)
Spices: **Mustard Seeds**,
**Cumin Seeds, Asafoetida,
Turmeric Powder, Curry
Leaves, Urad Dal, Ginger,
Pepper or Green Chillies** (as
required)
*(Various nutrients, including
Mg, Iron, F, AO)*

Homemade Masala Powder:
Cinnamon Stick
(1 finger size),
Bay Leaves (2)
Cloves (4)
Coriander Seeds (1
tablespoon),
Cumin Seeds
Star Anise
(Various nutrients)

Instructions

1. Cook the cannellini beans in a pot with enough water to prevent sticking, until they are soft.

2. In a separate pan, dry roast the spices (mustard seeds, cumin seeds, asafoetida, turmeric powder, curry leaves, urad dal, ginger, pepper or green chillies).

3. Add washed and cut gourd veg pieces to the pan. Steam along with the kale until both are soft.

4. Prepare the masala powder by grinding the cinnamon stick, bay leaves, cloves, coriander seeds, cumin seeds, and star anise.

5. Add a spoonful of this masala powder and a little water to the cooked cannellini beans to create a curry-like consistency.

6. Serve the curry with water-rich vegetables instead of rice for easy digestion.

Supports cardiovascular health and digestion with hydrating snake gourd and nutrient-rich kale, and offers a protein and fibre-packed, plant-based meal with cannellini beans for heart health and satiety.

Nutritious Drumstick Lentil Curry with Okra Fry

Ingredients

Whole Red Lentils (½ cup, washed and soaked)
(PbP, F, Iron, Mg)
Drumsticks (2, trimmed)
(VitC, Potassium, F)
Lady's Finger/Okra (200 gms)
(VitC, VitK, F, Mg)
Dill Leaves (A Small Bunch)
(VitC, Calcium, Iron)
Coriander Leaves (A Small Bunch)
(VitC, VitK, VitA, Iron)
Raw Mango (1, deseeded)
(VitC, VitA, Folate)
Green Chillies (4)
(VitC, VitB6, VitA)
Essential Spices:
Asafoetida, Turmeric Powder, Cumin Seeds, Curry Leaves, Ginger or Ginger Powder
Dulse (Seaweed, used as a salt alternative)
(Iodine, Potassium, Iron)

Instructions

1. Cook the soaked red lentils until soft.

2. In another pan, dry roast the essential spices and then add ginger and 2 sliced green chillies.

3. Add raw mango pieces and drumstick pieces to the spice mix. Cook with some water until soft.

4. Once the vegetables are cooked, add the cooked lentils. Use dulse as a salt alternative and garnish with dill leaves.

5. For the lady's finger fry, dry roast essential spices in a pan. Add washed and cut okra (with tails snipped off). Sprinkle a little water to prevent sticking and steam until soft.

6. Season the okra with dulse for flavour. Garnish with ground peanuts or hemp seeds and coriander leaves.

7. Serve the dal and lady's finger fry together as a hearty meal.

Hearty Cauliflower and Kale with Lentils

Ingredients

Green Lentils (½ cup, washed and soaked for 6-8 hours)
(PbP, F, Iron, Mg)

Cauliflower Florets
(Around 10)
(VitC, VitK, F, AO)

Kale Leaves (A Bunch)
(VitA, VitC, Calcium, Iron)

Essential Spices: Turmeric, Cumin Seeds, Pepper, Ginger, Dry Mango Powder Roasted Sesame Seeds Powder (1 tablespoon)
(Calcium, Mg, PbP)

Instructions

1. Steam the soaked green lentils until they are soft.

2. In a separate pan, steam the cauliflower florets and kale leaves with the essential spices (turmeric, cumin seeds, pepper, ginger, and dry mango powder) until they are tender.

3. Once cooked, serve the lentils and steamed vegetables together.

4. Sprinkle 1 tablespoon of roasted sesame seeds powder or your choice of seeds powder over the dish for added flavour and nutrition.

Boosts heart health and digestion with protein-rich green lentils, supports immune health with cauliflower's vitamins, and enhances bone health and blood formation with nutrient-dense kale, complemented by mineral-rich sesame seeds for a balanced, plant-based meal.

Recovery Remedies

Cold Remedies

Lemon, Ginger, and Raw Honey:

Combine grated ginger in hot water, let it cool to lukewarm, then add lemon juice and a spoon of raw honey. Consume 3-4 times daily for relief from cold symptoms.

Tulsi Turmeric Pepper and Ginger Tea:

In a pan, heat water with crushed ginger, turmeric powder, and tulsi leaves. Strain and consume as is, or add palm jaggery for taste.

Cough Relief

Clove Buds:

Sucking on 2 or 3 clove buds can help expel phlegm and clear cough.

Kashayam/Herbal Concoction:

Boil water with cumin seeds, peppercorns, turmeric, ginger, coriander seeds, and mint leaves. Reduce to half, strain, and consume with palm jaggery on an empty stomach.

Cabbage Soup:

Steep organic cabbage in hot water until softened. Drink the nutrient-rich water for cough relief.

Cinnamon Turmeric Water:

Mix ¼ teaspoon each of cinnamon and turmeric powder in lukewarm water. Add lemon and/or ginger for enhanced detox and antiseptic properties.

Immune Boosting and Detox

Green Leafy Juice:

Blend a choice of green leaves like coriander, mint, parsley, or basil with ginger, lemon juice, or gooseberry. Enjoy this nutrient-rich drink as a morning detox and immune booster.

Constipation Aid

Flaxseeds Water:

Soak 1 tablespoon of flaxseeds in a glass of water overnight. Filter and drink the water in the morning for relief from constipation.

Fever Management

Barley Water:

Dry roast and coarsely grind 1-2 tablespoons of barley. Boil water, add barley, and simmer until aromatic. Consume this throughout the day for fever management.

Recovery Remedies

Eye Problems and Asthma Relief

Dwarf Copper Leaves Juice:

Blend dwarf copper leaves with a piece of ginger, gooseberry, and water. Consume as a green juice drink for relief from eye problems and asthma.

Memory Enhancement

Brahmi Leaves Juice:

Chew fresh Brahmi leaves on an empty stomach or blend them with ginger, celery stalk, cucumber slice, and lemon juice. This juice aids in memory enhancement.

Neurological Health

Beet Carrot Juice with Ginger:

Blend peeled beetroot, carrots, and ginger. Consume the filtered juice with added water for neurological health benefits.

UTI - Urinary tract infection

Barley Water:

Dry roast barley grains, grind them coarsely, boil water, add the barley powder, simmer until aromatic, strain, and consume throughout the day.

Digestive Issues

CCF Tea (Cumin, Coriander, Fennel):

Brew a tea with equal parts of cumin, coriander, and fennel. Strain and drink to aid digestion.

Ajwain/Carom Seeds Drink:

Boil carom seeds in water, strain, and drink on an empty stomach for digestive relief.

Weight Management

For Weight Gain - Soaked Nuts and Fruits Shake:

Blend soaked nuts with your choice of fruits for a nutrient-rich shake.

For Losing Weight - Lemon Ginger Water:

Combine lemon and ginger in lukewarm water, drink in the morning for weight management.

For Losing Weight - Horse Gram Lentils Soup:

Cook soaked horse gram lentils, season with spices, and consume as a light soup.

General Wellness

Amla Juice:

Extract juice from amla (Indian gooseberry) for a vitamin C-rich drink.

Ash Gourd Juice:

Blend ash gourd with water, strain, and drink for hydration and nutrition.

Keymarkers in the Recipe

Here is the abbreviated list of nutritional elements commonly found in ingredients in the recipes mentioned across this book.

1. Macronutrients:

- **PbP**: Plant-Based Protein
- **F**: Fibre
- **C**: Carbohydrates
- **SF**: Saturated Fat
- **USF**: Unsaturated Fat

2. Vitamins:

VitA: Vitamin A

VitB1: Thiamin (Vitamin B1)

VitB2: Riboflavin (Vitamin B2)

VitB3: Niacin (Vitamin B3)

VitB5:Pantothenic Acid (Vitamin B5)

VitB6: Pyridoxine (Vitamin B6) -

VitB7:Biotin (Vitamin B7) -

VitB9:Folate (Vitamin B9)

VitB12:Cobalamin (Vitamin B12)

VitC: Vitamin C

VitD: Vitamin D

VitE: Vitamin E

VitK: Vitamin K

3. Minerals

Ca: Calcium

Iron *(Fe not used to avoid confusion with Fibre F)*

Mg: Magnesium

P: Phosphorus

K: Potassium

Na: Sodium

Zn: Zinc

Cu: Copper

Mn: Manganese

Se: Selenium

4. Other Nutrients

AO: Antioxidants

OMG3: Omega-3 Fatty Acids -

OMG6: Omega-6 Fatty Acids -

CL: Cholesterol

GF: Gluten-Free

LC: Low-Calorie

LF: Low-Fat

LS: Low-Sodium

Downloadable Charts

Enhance Your Journey

Take your exploration around holistic plant-based eating even further with these convenient visualized guides now just a scan away!

Food Combinations Chart

Quickly reference which plant-powered pairings promote optimal digestion and nutrient absorption versus what food friends tend to cause discomfort through this at-a-glance infographic guide extracted from "The Holistic Science of Combining Foods for Healing" reference eBook (available at Aanandham.uk).

Nourishing Food Replacement Chart

Substitute animal products, processed convenience items and commercially farmed products with more ethical, environmentally sustainable whole food options using this chart illustrating better choices for everything from meat to dairy.

Simply open your phone's camera app and point it at the designated QR code below to instantly access each educational bonus resource - no typing lengthy links required. Consider posting printouts of these infographics on your refrigerator or kitchen walls for handy assistance elevating nutrition!

SCAN ME

DOWNLOAD

GITA CHAPTER 9 VERSE 27

*yat karoṣi yad aśnāsi yaj
juhoṣi dadāsi yat
yat tapasyasi kaunteya tat
kuruṣva mad-arpaṇam*

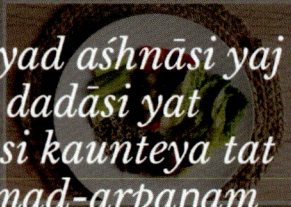

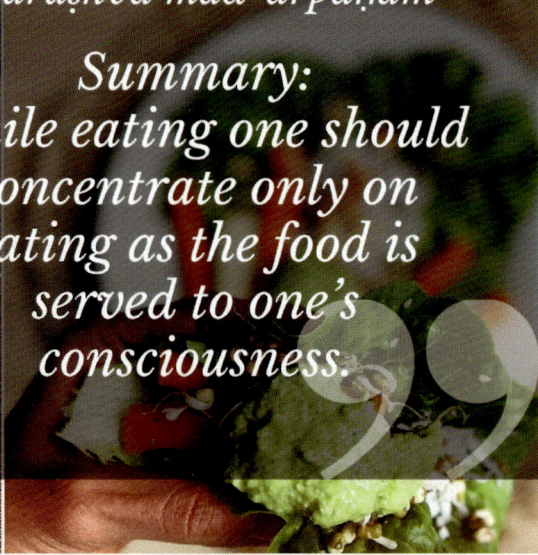

*Summary:
While eating one should
concentrate only on
eating as the food is
served to one's
consciousness.*

GITA CHAPTER 17 VERSE 8

*ayuh-sattva-balarogya-sukha-
priti-vivardhanah
rasyah snigdhah sthira hridya
aharah sattvika-priyah*

*Summary:
Satvic foods nourish both
body and spirit with
purity, strength and
natural vitality*

Let food be thy medicine and medicine be thy food

HIPPOCRATES